The Silent Mentor

The Journey of Discovering one's true purpose

The Silent Mentor

The Journey of Discovering one's true purpose

Mike Raber

Published by Centsible Publishing Inc.
Milwaukee Wisconsin USA

The Silent Mentor

The Journey of Discovering one's true purpose

Published by Centsible Publishing Inc.
Milwaukee Wisconsin USA

ISBN - 978-1-7334410-0-1 Paperback

Cover Design by:
Theresa Wilmot - Wilmot Designs

Interior Editing by:
Amy Oaks – Amy Oaks Writes

Ordering information

To order additional copies, call us at 414-559-7535 or e-mail us
at sales@thesilentmentor.com

Dedication

I dedicate this book to my loving wife for putting up with me all these years. To my amazing children for being such amazing kids and now young adults, who not only are on their own quest to make the world a better place, but have been an inspiration for me to follow. To my dad for sharing Christ with me when we would spend time together. The many great mentors God placed in my life, such as Brian, Dean, Dina, and Chad and to Roger for not only being one of the Godliest men that I know, but also a great friend who helped me through a very dark time in my life. Without all of you this book may never have come to life.

Table of Contents

"Your word is a lamp to my feet and a light to my path."

Acknowledgements

There are many people I want to thank, starting with my own family for teaching me values and the belief that I can do anything I put my mind to. Those beliefs gave me the strength to continue on when many of the people around me told me I was crazy for having such a dream.

I especially want to thank my wife Jennifer and our three lovely children for being by my side and for their contributions to the development of the many stories that I will share with you throughout this book.

My gratitude also goes to Sister Allen, who, when I was at a point in my life when I felt alone and lost, took me under her wing and helped rekindle an internal flame that had burned out. For that, she will always have a special place in my heart. Also, to Henry Chang and Ti-men for being amazing mentors, while teaching me the importance of perseverance. To Jennifer's parents for believing in me and allowing their youngest daughter to travel across the world with me. To JX Enterprises for allowing me as kid to play on the trucks at the Waukesha Peterbilt dealership. And to Rick Smith for giving me the opportunity to become part of the JXE family as an adult bringing a lifelong dream to realty.

And most of all, to my silent mentor, for guiding me through many journeys while reminding me to stay patient when I didn't want to, to stay true to my faith when I felt like the world was closing in on me, and to always, even at times when I least felt like it, have faith that in the end God will work all things out. It is for those reasons that I felt drawn to write this book.

"By ourselves we can do great things, yet together we can climb the highest mountains."
- Mike Raber 2017

INTRODUCTION

The creation of this book has been a culmination of a life-long dream to go out and positively impact people's lives through empowering them to live their lives on purpose. When it comes to living a purpose driven life, faith plays a big part in it.

Ever since I was young, I had a strong sense of faith that I was connected to something much larger than myself. As a teenager, I was given the vision of an entrepreneurial movement, or business community, created to empower people with the resources needed to design a great business and life while becoming the person God designed them to be. Over the years, it has been a long journey as I continue to develop and bring my dream of such an entrepreneurial community into reality.

My life has been an amazing adventure of different experiences, challenges, and eye-opening lessons that together shaped the man I have become. There were many times when I felt completely alone, yet through it all I felt very lucky because when times felt the hardest, it often felt like there was someone by my side; like a silent mentor guiding me when I needed it most.

As I compiled all the different stories and lessons, I decided to share them with you as a fictional story about a man named Sam who ended up sitting next to an older much wiser man named Pistis (which means faith in Greek) on a flight from Milwaukee to Seattle. Throughout the conversation, Pistis asks Sam questions, and Sam shares different stories while answering his questions. Pistis share many teaching points, leading up to a powerful revelation at the end of the book.

Granted, I changed the names of the people in the stories. Pistis is a fictional character representing my silent mentor, and Sam was my childhood nickname, hence using that name to represent myself. However, the stories are all true. It's my goal that as you read this book, the many adventures and stories of how 'by the grace of God', I was able to make split second choices that radically changed the course of my life. But most of all, I hope that these different stories and examples will show you that by staying true to your own faith, even when it feels like you're alone and nothing is working for you, you're never truly alone. It's so important to persevere and not give up. We are all here for a purpose or reason, and it's up to us to discover what that purpose is. God's true glory can shine through each of us if we only let Him.

Most of all, throughout this book, by using my own journey, I hope to show you how even the smallest choice or decision put in front of us can have a huge impact over not only our lives, but the lives of those around us. I also hope to show you the potential dangers of ignoring the warning signs or clues that are put in front of us.

The conversation between Pistis and Sam lays out the process like a road map, not only for me, but also for you to use in your own life story. Don't miss the directional arrows put in front of you each and every day.

It has taken the help of many great mentors. They helped keep me on track when I lost faith or focus, and they helped to shape the man, father, and leader that I have become. As I sit here thinking back on all the stories, I pray that they will help to inspire you to find your own greatness. Happy reading!

CHAPTER 1:

The Flight to Seattle

Relieved that I quickly made it through security, I opened a large white glass door, walked into the Sky Club, and smiled at a well-dressed lady sitting behind the counter. Looking up from a paper she was reading, she smiled and said, "Good afternoon sir, welcome to the club. Where are you flying to this afternoon?"

"I'm heading to Seattle," I replied as I handed her my boarding pass.

"I haven't seen you in here for a while," the lady said as she handed my boarding pass back to me.

"Yeah, it's been almost three months now."

"Wow, that's some break; you have been flying to Seattle every other week for a while now, haven't you?"

"Yeah, for the past three years anyway. But in August, my wife Jennifer and I packed up our son and daughter and got them off to college. Then, I took some personal time and took a ten-week very intensive truck driving course through the local community college, which has been a goal of mine since I was quite young."

"Do you work for a trucking company?" she asked.

"Nope, some guys like fast cars, others like boats. For me it's always been semi-trucks," I said, laughing.

"But now it's time to get back to reality. So, here I am once again on my way to Seattle for a few days of meetings."

"Well, it's nice to have you back in the club. I hope you have a safe and prosperous trip," She said with a large smile.

"Thanks," I said smiling back, then walked to the back of the club, got a bowl of soup, something to drink and sat down.

'Well, here I am once again sitting here waiting to board my flight to Seattle. If only it was practical to drive there; I really hate flying,' I thought to myself.

A short time later, a voiced echoed over the intercom, "Ladies and gentlemen, flight 1995 to Seattle is now getting ready to board."

I gathered my stuff, stood up, and walked over to where people were getting ready to board. A few minutes later, I entered the jet way and walked onto the plane.

'Well no turning back now, next stop Minneapolis, then on to Seattle. At least I have my favorite seat on the flight,' I thought to myself, as I sat down in seat 2D.

I settled into my seat and took a sip of water from the small water bottle that was there waiting for me. The afternoon sky was bright blue with a few soft white clouds off on the horizon. I heard the sound of the aircraft door being closed and locked as an older gentleman sat down next to me. He smiled and said, "Hi my name is Pistis," and wished me a good afternoon.

"Hi, my name is Sam," I replied.

There was something so familiar about the gentleman. I had never seen him before, yet somehow, I felt like I knew him. The plane slowly edged backwards as we pulled away from the gate. The whine of the jet engines echoed throughout the plane as it headed down the runway.

The day was turning out to be successful despite the fact that I was once again on an airplane. I sat back in my seat and took another sip of water as I closed my eyes, and said a small prayer - one that I have grown accustomed to saying every time I take off:

"Lord please keep your hand under this plane and bring us into Minneapolis safely and smoothly. Then please be with the next flight protecting the plane once again, keeping your hand under it so that we have a smooth and safe flight into Seattle. And Lord please bless my time in Seattle so that I am able to fulfill the reasons why I'm there and allow me to bless those you put in front of me. Please help make this a successful week, so that when I return home, I can tell Jennifer and the kids that the trip and my time away from them wasn't in vain. In Jesus name, Amen."

Opening my eyes, I looked out the window as the plane started to lift away from the ground, away from all that seemed safe. The plane flew higher and higher; the airport and city become part of the past. Once again asking God to bless the trip, I took another sip of water.

"There are not many times in life when there is an obvious breaking point between the past and the present, but taking off and watching the ground disappear into the horizon sure seems to be one of them," Pistis said, as I sat there looking out the window.

"Are you headed to Minneapolis or going somewhere else?" Pistis asked.

"I'm headed to Seattle," I replied.

"Ah Seattle the Emerald city; one of my favorite cities. Are you from Seattle?"

"No, I lived there for 16 years but I grew up in Milwaukee."

Pistis and I talked for a while, then I pulled out my note pad and wrote down some thoughts about the last couple of months. So many things had happened since I walked off the last plane after returning to Milwaukee from Seattle. Three months had been the longest I'd been away from Seattle in four years.

Sitting back and taking another sip from the small water bottle, I thought about all that had happened over the last four years, and an incredible sense of sadness came over me. Here I was on my way back to Seattle, only this time things seemed so different. Everything I knew to be true in Seattle no longer was. Everything I knew to be familiar at home was quickly moving into a new season of life. My wife Jennifer and I had joined the empty nesters club; no one at home now to greet us except for Lucy, our dog.

Looking over at me Pistis smiled as he said, "You look like you have a lot on your mind. Is that why you're writing so many notes?"

"Yeah, sometimes I find that when I'm not able to talk about things, if I write it helps to clear my mind," I replied.

"Writing our thoughts down, or journaling, can be a very powerful tool for organizing thoughts," Pistis said, still smiling.

Just then, the pilot announced that we were on final descent and would be landing in Minneapolis shortly. After a few minutes, the plane landed and taxied to the terminal. Pistis turned to me and said it was nice talking with me and that he hoped to see me on another flight.

"Thanks, same to you," I replied.

We got off the plane and I headed to the Sky Club so I could get something to eat before the next flight. About five minutes before it was time to board, I got up and walked to my gate. When it was my time to board, I walked onto the plane and sat down once again in 2D, opening the bottle of water that was once again sitting there waiting for me. Lo and behold, Pistis boarded the plane and sat down next to me.

"We meet again," he said with a smile as he sat down. "Yeah, what a coincidence," I replied, surprised yet pleased.

"Some might find it a coincidence that you and I are sitting next to each other two flights in a row. However, I find that in life there are very few coincidences. Rather, they happen for reasons we do not yet understand," Pistis said, smiling.

"True, but this is the first time it has happened to me and I fly quite a bit," I said.

"Sometimes it's the very things that seem out of place or odd that makes the most sense in life. True, you could call it a coincidence, or maybe there is a reason for us to be sitting together on this flight. You tell me," Pistis replied with a large smile.

"I guess stranger things have happened," I said, smiling.

"So, what brings you to Seattle?"

"It's a long story," I replied.

"Well, from what you were sharing with me on the last flight, something tells me it's a story worth hearing. Lucky for me, we have lots of time before we land," Pistis said, chuckling.

"To be honest, I'm not even sure where to begin."

"Well, how about starting with 'once upon a time in a place long long ago, there lived a young boy named Sam'," Pistis said smiling.

"Nah, too cliché," I replied.

"Ok then, how about 'In a land far far away'?"

"Nope too much like a children's book."

"Well, what about just starting with why you're going to Seattle?"

"Yeah, I guess that would be a good place to begin."

"So, as I was telling you on our way to Minneapolis, we used to live in Seattle and then moved back to Milwaukee in 2005 so we could be closer to family. Yet, part of Seattle had grown on me. As my oldest daughter was looking at colleges, things were looking like she may end up going to the University of British Columbia just outside of Vancouver, BC. My son was looking at the University of Washington, so I set a goal to open a branch office in Seattle. The funny thing is neither of them ended up going to school there."

"So, did you decide to open a branch office there anyway?" Pistis asked.

"Yeah, we have a small office in Tacoma and another one in Bellevue. That's a funny story in its own right."

"We still have a lot of flying time. So, continue."

"Ok then, I'm not sure if you're a person of faith or not, but …"

"Well they do call me Pistis," Pistis laughed.

Not completely sure what Pistis meant, I began the story. "Ok, so Sabrina and I were touring the University of British Columbia, and I set the goal to open a branch office within six months. I didn't know why, but it felt right. I prayed that if it was indeed the right move, then an opportunity would arise for it to happen. A week after Sabrina and I got back to Milwaukee, I went into the president of our firm's office and told him about my goal.

Chuckling, Dave, our firm's president said, 'It's funny you say that because I just a call from a guy named Robert who lives in Seattle. He heard about our firm and wants to join us. He is coming to our annual event next month.'

'Really? I want to meet him.'

'I can introduce you two, but I doubt you know him. Seattle is a pretty big place,' Dave said smiling.

'Of course, I probably don't know him, but I want to.'

'Ok, I'll introduce you two at the event.'

'Great thanks Dave.'

The morning of the event, I pulled into the parking lot and said a quick prayer, 'If this is the right time and decision to open a branch office, then please let my meeting with Robert go well.' I walked into the event, put my notepad down on a table, then walked around trying to find Robert. It came time for the event to begin, and still no sight of Robert, so I gave up and sat down. There were around 120 people in the room, so I knew he had to be there … but where?

I sat down and introduced myself to an unknown man sitting next to me.

'Hi, my name is Sam, are you new to the firm?'

'Hi, my name is Robert, I'm from Seattle. Yes, I joined the firm two days ago,' he said.

'You're not going to believe this, but I just spent the last 25 minutes trying to find you,' I replied.

'You spent the last 25 minutes trying to find me? But why??'

'This is going to sound crazy, but last month I told Dave that I set a goal to open a branch office in Seattle. And he told me about your phone conversation and that you were coming today.'

'Wow! Robert said laughing, then this too will sound crazy. After I came in and put my stuff down, I went back up to my room and called my wife. She told me to pray that God would bring someone into my life during today's event that could help me open an office in Seattle. If that is truly God's calling, it appears that my prayer may have been answered.'

'We have so much to talk about. I'm going to be in Seattle next week. Would you like to meet for coffee?' I replied.

'That would be great; I'm looking forward to it,' Robert replied.

So, Robert and I met for coffee the following week in Seattle, and it was obvious to us that we both had very similar goals. We then sat down and made a plan for opening an office in downtown Bellevue. Six months later we had the first branch office in the Seattle area. It was just large enough for three desks and had a small conference room next door. Now all we had to do was grow it, which meant that we would need both clients and advisors."

"Wow, that's some story. It's amazing how you two met," Pistis replied, smiling.

"You can say that again. And how we met is only the half of it."

"Well then, please continue."

"A year and a half after we opened the branch office in Bellevue, we recruited three agents who helped us grow the office and had a handful of clients. One afternoon, Robert and I were sitting in the office talking, and I asked him why he went from being a Boeing engineer to becoming a financial advisor.

He explained, 'Well about ten years ago, a friend from church invited me to go with him to a Toastmasters meeting where people gave speeches on different topics. During the meeting, an eight-year-old girl gave a speech on why it's so important for parents to teach financial management skills to their kids. She really impressed me with her passion. A few days after leaving the meeting, I kept thinking about her message. I was sharing her message with my wife, Ann, and she suggested that since I was getting ready to retire from Boeing, maybe I should become a financial advisor so I could help in her cause by educating families on the importance of financial planning, and teaching core financial skills to the children in their lives. I have been on a mission to do that ever since.'

I couldn't believe what I was hearing. Ten years ago, an eight-year-old girl moved Robert to the point of making a career change in order to help the girl fulfill her mission. He then ended up joining our firm. Then, Robert and I opened a branch office together ten years later, 2,000 miles away from where I was living at the time. I sat there trying to keep my eyes from tearing up.

'Are you ok?' Robert asked.

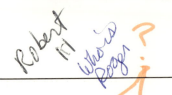

Regaining my composure, I smiled and said, 'Yeah, it's just that, do you know who that eight-year-old girl was?'

'No, I never saw her again after that day,' Roger replied with a strange look on his face.

'She was my daughter, and that was the last Toastmasters meeting we went to before we moved back to Wisconsin.'

We both sat there silently for a few minutes. Then Roger smiled and noted, 'God sure works in funny ways.'

'He sure does,' I said.

I knew then that my being in Seattle and my desire to build a branch office there couldn't have been more right. I spent the next year helping Robert with the Bellevue office. I had a vision of designing entrepreneurial communities throughout the country. So along with helping Robert in Seattle, over the next year, I went to many different seminars around the country in search of people who wanted to help with my vision.

December 2013, I was invited to attend a retreat that was taking place in March of 2014. At first, I was elated since only 200 people out of a coaching community of 6,000 get invited to this event. Yet here I was. I had the golden ticket.

The only challenge was that the retreat cost $5,000 and would involve spending three days in San Diego.

I was so excited, but then reality started to set in. Why should I to go to this retreat? After all, I didn't have $5,000 to spend no matter how great it was. Everyone there had successful businesses whereas I was struggling at best. But then again, I was invited. So, someone believed that I deserved to be there!

After praying for direction, I knew deep down that if I could meet just one person there who shared similar goals, then it would somehow all work out in the end. So picked up my phone, called Buffini and Company and registered for the event.

It was now the beginning of March and I was still having second thoughts about going to the retreat. It seemed so right, but I still couldn't justify it given my current financial state.

Once again, I put my head down on my desk and prayed for direction. I prayed for the introduction to just one person that could help me move my business to the next level. I felt this sense of peace come over me. Three days later, I boarded a flight from Seattle to San Diego. The first day of the retreat went really well. The speaker was incredibly motivating and the networking was great. I saw many colleagues. Some were past clients; others were people I had met at different events.

At dinner we broke up into different groups for some exercises. The group leader had us go around the table, introduce ourselves, state our purpose for being there, and divulge our goals for the next five years.

Ron, a gentleman sitting next to me who was also from Seattle, had a moving story. I wanted to learn more about what he was doing, and for some strange reason I believed that he was the person I had been praying about. So, after the meeting, I asked him if he would like to meet for coffee the following week.

We met at a coffee shop in Seattle a week later and had a great conversation about business, his past, and why he had decided to go into real estate. I told him I was building a branch office in Seattle and I thought it may be just what he was looking for. About nine months later he joined our firm. Soon after, he ran our Tacoma branch and we had become friends."

"Wow, that's some story. But tell me, why do you pray for something and then say it's strange or crazy when you get what you were praying for? Don't you believe you're worthy of getting your prayers answered?" Pistis asked.

"I guess it's just the *way* it happens; a feeling of complete peace always comes over me. The situation feels so right," I said.

"Perhaps what you're feeling is the presence of the Holy Spirit working within you."

"I guess. It just seems to happen so effortlessly," I replied.

"What do you mean by effortlessly?" Pistis asked.

"Like my sitting down next to Robert at the annual conference. Or how in a room of 200 people, I ended up sitting next to Ron at dinner. Then we end up being in the same small group of seven people over the next two days."

"True, that part seems easy. But don't forget that you had to make the decision to go to the retreat when you had every reason not to. Or how once you made the decision to go, you then prayed about it and asked God to bring someone into your life who could help you; an act of faith that many people wouldn't demonstrate. Did you expect that the person would float into the room on a cloud?" Pistis asked, smiling.

"No of course not. I don't know, I guess it just seems like such a coincidence," I replied.

"Chuckling, Pistis said, "There you go again using that word. One person's coincidence is often another's answer to prayer. It's just that sometimes we might not know that we prayed for it to happen."

"How can you pray for something without knowing that you prayed for it?" I asked.

"Have you ever set a goal for something and then went to work at trying to accomplish your goal, knowing that as much as you wanted the outcome, you were open to another outcome if it was better than your original goal?"

"Yeah, I guess so."

"Ok, now have you ever said a prayer for a certain outcome, and ended the prayer with "In Jesus' name, Amen?""

"Yes, all the time, that is how I was taught to end a prayer."

"And why is that do you suppose?"

"I guess it's because when I say a prayer, no matter how much I want my prayer to be heard, God may have a better plan."

"Correction Sam, your prayers are always heard; they just aren't always answered in the way you were hoping. Sometimes the answer is yes, sometimes it's not now, sometimes it's slow, and sometimes there is something even better. You're just not ready for it yet. However, in time - when and if you're ready - the answer will show itself. But they are always heard."

"So, if I understand what you're saying; when I set a goal and go to work on reaching that goal, knowing that ultimately I don't have complete control over the outcome, or at least the timing of the outcome, it's like praying?" I asked.

"Not exactly. When you pray, you're having a conversation with God. When you set a goal and work to achieve it, you're putting your intention out there; what some might refer to as the law of attraction. It then starts to take on energy of its own.

It's when you are willing *not* to reach your desired outcome, if there is a better outcome for you, then forms the true power which will manifest the outcome. When you put it to prayer, you're able to smoothly draw or attract such things into your life; your so-called coincidences.

I might argue that a coincidence is really unnoticed or misguided direction. All people have a purpose or design for their lives, but they rarely pay attention to it. They set out to accomplish or experience something, yet their focus is on something totally different. Then when their actions bring about the experience, they are surprised and call it a coincidence."

"Do you mean like God's plan for us?" I asked.

"In a way, one might argue that God has a plan for us, yet because of free will, people have the ability to change the direction of their lives. That's why it's so important to listen for God's direction through prayer. You and your wife probably had a plan for the direction you wanted your kids to go in. But I would be willing to bet they didn't grow into, or follow, the exact plan you had. Because of free will, like your kids, people have the ability to move away from God's plan or their true purposes. That's why prayer and meditation are so important. They help people live in the present. It is by being in the present that people are able to get in touch with their true purposes."

"I see. So, when I get a nudge to move in a certain direction, it's because the path is being revealed to me."

"Correct."

"Why is it so hard for people to see, or discover, their destinies?" I asked.

"It's because they get caught up in the busyness of their lives. People miss the clues that are presented to them. The objective isn't so much as blindly following some path, or bouncing from place to place, rather continually searching for one's purpose, or what people might call their destinies. You're lucky because it seems you're able to recognize the signs when they are shown to you," Pistis replied.

"The crazy thing, or I guess amazing thing, is that I have always had an inner source of faith that I have had someone by my side guiding me and at times keeping me out of trouble. I guess kind of like what someone might refer to as a guardian angel. In my case, however, it is more like an invisible friend or silent mentor. In a way it's been a blessing. Many times, it's more like a curse."

"Why do you say that?" Pistis asked

"Because, I will get a nudge to do something, or hear what sounds like someone from behind me, tell me to do something that makes no sense at the time," I replied.

"Your invisible friend?" Pistis asked.

"Yeah, I guess? Anyway, it often causes those around me to think I've lost it."

"Yet you still listen to the voice, when most people would simply ignore it?" Pistis said smiling.

"So, tell me then, when you listen to the voice, do bad things happen because you're listening to it?" Pistis asked.

"No, my listening to that voice is usually the beginning of something great. And, often times it comes right before, or right after, something happens that totally turns my life upside down."

Just then the flight attendant leaned over us and asked if we wanted a grilled chicken salad or beef short ribs for dinner. I got the short ribs and Pistis had the salad.

The Lord is my shepherd, I shall
not want, He makes me lie down
in green pastures, He leads me
beside quiet waters, He restores
my soul. He guides me in paths
of righteousness for his name's
sake. Even though I walk
through the valley of the shadow
of death, I will fear no evil, for
You are with me; your rod and
your staff, they comfort me.
Psalm 23:1-4

"I can do all things through Him who strengthens me. – Philippians 4:13

CHAPTER 2:

Overcoming Challenges

The flight attendant brought us our food. Pistis, after swallowing a bite of his salad, looked over at me and said, "It sounds like you were taught some great lessons on staying true to your faith when Overcoming Challenges. What are some different challenges that you had to face growing up, and how, with God's help, were you able to overcome them?"

"It's funny you ask, because that has been a common theme throughout my life."

"What do you mean?"

"Well, it often seems that I am put in situations that appear nearly impossible to overcome. Then, just as I'm about to give up, someone enters my life who is able to help guide me through it."

"Yeah, that is more common than people realize. Often, in order for God to truly work in our lives, we have to reach the point at which we are ready to learn. Just like when you're exercising, you have to push your body or work a muscle to the point of failure. It is at that point the muscle is able to grow stronger. The brain works the same way. By being pushed almost to the breaking point, it is able to truly develop mental toughness and tenacity.

People might say they have lived a hard life and become resentful or full of self-pity. Yet, if they really examined their lives, they would often find that life has ups and downs, but in the end, as with most things, ultimately it comes down to our reactions to bad or good things when they happen that determines the final outcome. Self-talk, or how people view outside influences, will determine their reactions to any given situation. Do they view it as something they have some control over, or something that simply happens to them? If they believe they have control over something that happens to them, they will have a more positive reaction.

Whereas if they don't think they have any control over something that happens to them, they will feel like victims. Over time, they may even begin to expect the worst before anything ever happens. Granted, sometimes bad things just happen outside of people's control. But overall, it's important that people try their best to embrace the pain and persevere through life's challenges. This is where true mental growth comes from. The more people are able to persevere through hard times, the easier it will be to empathize with, and therefore bless, those around them."

"So, in a way, it's not so much the challenge, rather how we react to the challenge, that truly shapes us?" I asked.

"Correct, just like the weightlifter who's trying to build up his biceps. Except in this case, it's the building of character, perseverance, integrity, and the list goes on. So anyway, back to my question. What are some different challenges you had to face growing up, and what did you learn from them?"

"Well, I guess one was that by the time I was two, my mom and dad decided to go their separate ways. I remember one night as my mom was getting ready for work, my dad sat down on the edge of a bed with my sister and me on either side of him. He told us that he had to go away for a while and wouldn't be able to see us, but that he would try to come back and see us whenever he could. Because I was so young, I didn't really know what was happening, yet I still seemed to feel a great loss in my life.

Two years later my mom married a man she worked with named John, who then stepped into the stepfather role. Over the next couple of years, my stepfather and I became very close. When I was five, I became best friends with a kid who lived across the alley from us. His family was Catholic and would invite me to go to church with them once in a while. I was fascinated by all the stories in the Bible. But, the most amazing thing was that I felt so at home there. Every time I entered the church and saw the cross hanging on the wall, I felt this huge sense of peace come over me.

My stepfather was interested in philosophy and we would talk about many different ideas. I would tell him things I had heard at my friend's church, and we would discuss them. He didn't believe in God, but respected many of the ideas we talked about. I learned many great things from my stepfather, but most of all, I learned to trust my inner-most feelings.

Besides being my stepfather, John became a great teacher in many ways. He was always trying to find ways to teach me how to become self-sufficient. I remember like it was yesterday, being five years old and having to practice Taekwondo two hours a day until my legs hurt. John would say I needed to learn how to defend myself. I would start crying and tell him that I wanted to stop, and he would say, "Sam I can't always be with you, and I need to know that you are able to defend yourself if you should ever need to."

'Ok,' I would say, wiping the tears away.

On the weekends we would go camping and he would show me how to start a fire by rubbing two sticks together, or how to set up camp, so our food would be safe from other animals. Or sometimes he would only bring a knife, some garbage bags, rope, and a few cans of food, and we would have to build a tent with the garbage bags and rope, use the knife to open the cans, or even cut firewood with the knife. He would say you might not have an axe or a tent, but a sharp knife, if properly used, can go a long way. Plus, you can find the necessary supplies anywhere.

He would often tell me that the trick to survival was knowing how to make do with your current environment; that nature was designed for the survival of all the different animals. So, everything we need for survival is around us, if we only know what to look for and where to look for it."

"Sounds like he was a great mentor for you as a young boy," Pistis replied, smiling.

"Yep, he had a way of taking almost anything and turning it into a life lesson. As an example, I remember one day when I was seven, Matt, my best friend at the time, and I were playing in my backyard.

'Hey, follow me up this tree!' Matt yelled out.

'Follow you where?' I responded.

'Up this tree! I'll bet we can make it all the way up to the top!' Matt yelled back. 'Ok, here I come!' Left, right, left, right, up the tree we went. I could see the top of the tree just a few feet away. Matt had already reached the top, and was sitting on a long, thick branch.

'Here I come!' I yelled up to him. Swoosh! Just then a rock flew past my head, almost knocking me out of the tree.

'Hey! Who did that?' I yelled down towards the ground.

'I did you dumb punk!' he yelled back.

'What? Are you Crazy?! You almost knocked me out of the tree!'

'Too bad I missed you!' Bruce Sprewer, a neighbor kid who lived half-way down the block, yelled back.

'What? When I get down out of this tree you will be sorry!' I yelled out.

'Yeah, screw you, you dumb punk!', the voice echoed back.

'Hey Matt, I need to take care of this! I'll see you on the ground!' I yelled up to Matt. I quickly climbed down the tree and ran into the alley where Bruce was standing. 'Why did you throw the rock? I almost fell out of the tree!' I yelled at Bruce.

'What do you want? You dumb punk!' Bruce yelled at me. 'You'd better run back to where you came from, or I will whip your punk butt.' He yelled.

'What do you mean by asking 'What do I want?' Why did you throw that rock at me? You almost knocked me out of the tree!' I yelled back.

'Yeah, too bad I missed. It would have been fun to watch your dumb butt fall out of that tree,' Bruce yelled. Something inside of me snapped, I wound up and hit Bruce as hard as I could, knocking him down. Bruce jumped up and ran back to his house as fast as he could. Matt came walking out into the alley and said that he was going home. 'What? Really, now? Ok.' Matt and I walked back to his house. A little while later, as I was crossing the alley to go back to my yard, I turned and saw Bruce and what looked like the rest of his family running down the alley towards me.

'You're dead!' They were yelling at me. 'Just wait till we get you.'

I ran into my yard as fast as I could and ran up on to my porch just as I felt someone punch me in the back. I whipped the porch door open and ran into the house and into the living room.

'Get back out here,' the kid who just hit me yelled out. 'We will show you that you can never hit our little brother.' 'Who do you think you are?' the kid yelled even louder. As I entered the living room, John turned his chair towards me and asked what all the commotion was about. I explained to him what had just happened.

'They're crazy! I'm not going out there. They will kill me!' I said with a loud sigh.

'Kill you!', he said laughing. 'Don't you think that's a little dramatic?'

'Dramatic! Are you serious? And what's worse, they started it. Bruce threw a rock at me almost knocking me out of the tree!' I said with tears running down my cheeks.

'Yeah, I heard them, so now what?' John replied.

'What do you mean now what?' I snapped back. 'Now I'm going to stay in here until they go home.'

'Ah! Hide in here until they go home,' John replied. 'Good plan, and what about tomorrow?'

'What do you mean, what about tomorrow? Tomorrow is another day.'

'So, you think they will simply just forget it about it?' John asked.

'Well I didn't think that far, but why not?' I said

'Well, I remember in the service we had a saying that goes A bullet may not have a memory, but if it's meant for you, the only way around it is to face it head on,' John replied.

'How do you face a bullet head on?' I asked.

Smiling, John said, 'It's a metaphor for facing your enemy head on. We can't control tomorrow. We can only control today. More so, we can only control right now. The choices we make in the present will ultimately affect the results we experience moving forward. As an example, let's say you're walking down the street and there are three kids coming at you who you know will beat you up if they catch you. You could turn and try running away. But since there are three of them, they will likely catch you, and from behind, which would put you in a bad place for defending yourself. Or, the better choice would be to look for the biggest kid, walk towards that kid, and as soon as they start to attack you, you punch the biggest kid knocking him down, then turn towards the next biggest kid and so on. Chances are once the other two see you knock the biggest kid down they will think twice before they try to attack you. They will expect you to run, and when you don't, it will make you a much more dangerous target.'

'I see, but what does that have to do with our neighbors wanting to kill me?' I asked.

'It's simple. Tomorrow, if they see you outside playing, they will still want to kill you, and you will likely be by yourself. Whereas, right now I can come with you to deal with this and make sure that you're all right.'

'Ok, so if I get this straight. The bullet is the Sprewers, and if I go out there now and face them, you will come with me and make sure that the bullet isn't a kill shot.'

'Exactly. By going out there now, I will make sure we resolve this situation.'

'Well, why don't you just go out there and tell them to go home and if they mess with me again, you will grab your 45 and end them,' I asked.

'True; on the surface, that may seem like a great idea, but then what? Say they get you tomorrow when you're by yourself, I grab my 45, and as you said, 'End Bruce.' Then his older sister grabs a gun and comes back after me. When does it end? And how many people will get hurt along the way? If you choose to do nothing, you still have to grow up in this neighborhood. And they will still want to beat you up.'

'I guess I didn't think that far,' I replied again.

'Whereas, what if you won their respect, and they became your friends? An enemy who respects you is far better than one who fears or hates you,' John said.

'I don't understand what you mean.'

'Ok, let's say you have two enemies. One doesn't like you and may even want to take you down. If he respects you for your power, integrity, or strength, he will most likely choose to co-exist with you. Whereas, if the other enemy doesn't like or respect you and wants to take you down, he will spend a great amount of time trying to weaken your power or try to find a way to quickly get rid of you out of fear that if he doesn't, you will come after him first, no matter what your intentions are.' John answered.

'But what does that have to do with me? They don't respect me or fear me. They just want to beat me up. And they started it!'

'I know it sounds strange, but force begets force. Yes, Bruce threw the rock at you, but it didn't hit you. You climbed down and hit him. So, in the end it's you who made the first contact. You hit Bruce and knocked him down. So, he and his family want to make you pay. Yes, Bruce threw the rock, but he didn't hit you with it. So right now, even though you think that you have a good reason, you're the aggressor, not Bruce.'

'That's stupid! What if he had hit me and I fell out of the tree? I could have been killed. He even said that he wished he had hit me!' I snapped back.

'True, but did you fall out of the tree?'

'What's that got to do with anything? I could have, and that's all that matters,' I replied angrily,

'No not really. You hit Bruce and now they want to teach you a lesson. No more, no less.' John said.

'Well that sucks! What did I do to bring this on? I was peacefully playing with Matt in the tree, in my own back yard.'

'True, but you climbed down out of the tree, walked out into the alley, and hit Bruce in the chest knocking him down. When you chose to hit Bruce, you set the ball in motion. You could have ignored him, or you and Matt could have climbed down out of the tree and come inside. Remember what I was saying about how the choices you make will determine the end result? The question now is, what are you going to do next? They are still outside. They still want to beat you up and will most likely want to tomorrow as well.'

'So, what do I do then?' I asked with tears starting to run down my cheeks again.

'Let's go out there and see what they think would be a fair way to resolve this,' John said.

'Ok then, let's go,' I said.

John and I got up and walked out into the yard. By now they had moved into the alley and some were headed down the alley on their way home. Bruce's older sister saw us coming towards them and called the rest to come back. We walked down the six stairs from our yard into the alley, and John asked Bruce's older sister what she thought would be a fair way to resolve this.

'Simple, we're going to beat his punk-self up so he never hits one of my brothers again!' she snapped back."

'So, you're saying Sam and Bruce should fight?' John said.

'No, your punk son is seven and Bruce is only six. We're all going to teach him a lesson.' Bruce's sister snapped back.

Laughing, John said, 'And how is that fair? One kid against nine? No, I don't think so. You'd better have a better suggestion, or this conversation is over.' John leaned forward towards Bruce's sister who was clearly running the circus, lowered his voice, looked Bruce's older sister in the eyes and said, 'We gave you a chance to resolve this fairly. If we turn around, go back inside, and you or one of your siblings messes with Sam some other time, I will make sure YOU will wish you never started this! Do you understand what I'm saying? I'm DONE playing around and your family is DONE scaring my son!'

'Excuse me, who do you think you are? There are nine of us and two of you. Plus, we have a large family. You'd better watch who you're talking to!'

'Sis, see that tattoo on his arm? I've seen it before on TV. I think it's some special forces Tattoo. You don't want him coming after us.' Bruce's older brother said.

22

'Do you have a suggestion or are we finished?' John said.

'Your punk son hit Bruce, so we need to make it right. Bruce is younger than him. So, he had no business hitting him. Bruce is only six. How about this: Tyrone is also six, Reggie is five, and Tony is four. Say your punk son fights those four. First one to quit loses.' Bruce's sister said with a snarl.

'Wait, I what?? You're crazy? How is that fair?' I asked.

'Fair! What you mean fair? You hit Bruce first.' Bruce's sister snapped back.

'Enough.' John said. 'Sam will fight the four youngest then when this is over, you or anyone in your family will never mess with him again. You got it!'

'Got it!' Bruce's sister replied.

'Yeah right! I hit Bruce because he almost knocked me out of a tree, then laughed about it. And now I'm supposed to fight Bruce and his three brothers? I don't think so! I'm not going to do it! That's it; I'm going back inside.' I yelled as I turned and started to walk towards the gate to my yard.

'You ain't leaving until we beat you bloody.' Bruce yelled.

'Wait, you're going to do what?' I thought to myself while turning and staring at Bruce in complete disbelief. 'I didn't do anything. I was peacefully playing in my back yard and you threw a rock at me, almost knocking me out of the tree. So, I hit you; so what? You deserved it! You started it, and now you want to beat me bloody! No, I don't think so. That's not how it works!' I yelled as loud as I could, then turned and punched Bruce right in the nose, once again knocking him down.

Just then, Tony threw a punch at me while Reggie tried to kick the side of my leg. Turning towards Tony, I blocked his punch and pushed him away while punching the top of Reggie's leg as it struck mine. Just then Willie jumped on my back and Tyrone threw a punch with his right hand toward my face. Grabbing Willie's hair, I flung him over my shoulder in Tyrone's direction just barely missing his punch. The older sister caught Reggie and pushed him towards me. Bruce jumped on my back, as Tony punched me in the stomach knocking me to the ground.

Pushing Bruce off my back, I jumped up and kicked Willie in the back with a spin kick, as he tried to punch me again.

I had had enough. I quickly ran towards the gate as John put his leg across the gate so I couldn't get past. John then said just loud enough for me to hear, 'The bullet still has your name on it. Turn around and finish it!'

'What?!' Shock, surprise, and a half a dozen other emotions hit me like a ton of bricks! As I turned to move back into the alley, I got punched in the face by Willie and kicked in the side by Tyrone. Stumbling sideways, Bruce once again jumped on my back and Reggie grabbed my shirt so he could push me to the ground. All I remember was seeing red, catching my balance while throwing a right hook kick hitting Reggie in the stomach, and following up with a left straight punch connecting with Reggie's nose. Blood gushed from his nose as he fell to the ground. Turning and blocking Bruce's elbow with my shoulder I pulled him from my back while striking him in the nose. As Bruce fell to the ground, I felt a sharp pain as I was kicked in the side by Willie. Tyrone grabbed my hair and I threw a right straight punch hitting him in the nose, causing it to bleed as he stumbled back and threw a right jab and a left straight punch striking Willie in the nose also causing it to bleed.

As everyone got to their feet, it was as if time had slowed way down. All five of us stood there looking at each other. We were all muddy. We were all bloody, and we were all crying.

'Please please, enough!' Bruce and Willie cried out, 'We want to go Home.'

'Ok, it's over!' The older sister shouted.

We all turned and walked in different directions. Finally, it was over, I was free. Happy it was over; John and I went back into the house. I took off my muddy, bloodied clothes, and took a long hot shower, glad that I had stared the bullet in the face."

"Wow! What a great learning opportunity. You learned many life lessons that day," Pistis replied, taking a sip of water.

"True, it's amazing how the decisions we make, even at such a young age, will and can radically affect our long term and short term outcomes. I remember how six months or so later, I was at the neighborhood pool. I was in the locker room getting dressed when three bigger kids came up to me and started to harass me. One of the kids said,

'Hey punk, where you going with my jacket?'

'Yeah, where you going with my pants?', another kid said. I started to think to myself, 'How am I going to get myself out of this?' Just then from across the room I heard,

'Hey, why you messing with our brother? You mess with him you mess with us.' To my surprise, there standing by the door were the Sprewer brothers.

'Oh, sorry, we just playing with the boy. We don't mean nothing by it,', one of the kids answered as they quickly left the locker room.

'You ok bro?' Bruce called out. 'Why don't you walk home with us?'

'Yeah, we will keep you safe,' Tyrone responded.

'Yeah, I'm fine, thanks guys,' I answered.

'No worries,' Bruce said. 'You're ok with us; we will always have your back. You're one of our brothers now.'

We didn't hang out and would often go weeks without seeing each other, but when we did, there was always that day in the alley. From that day on, a strong yet strange bond had formed between us.

I learned many great lessons from John. However, probably the biggest one, was to stay true to my inner voice and have faith that I had the ability to do great things in life. That when things seemed impossible, someone would show up to help make things better. I learned that sometimes I would have to push past pain, push past fear, push past my own self-doubt, and in the end, I would become stronger for it. Most importantly, I learned it was okay to dream, because even if things didn't turn out the way I had pictured, they would still be better than before. Most importantly, I learned that through faith anything is possible."

"Ah yes, Matthew 17:20-21, 'I tell all of you with certainty, If you have faith like a grain of a mustard seed, you can say to this mountain, 'move from here to there' and it will move,'" Pistis said smiling.

Wow, that sure was quite a lesson for such a young boy to learn." Pistis went on.

"Yeah, John seemed determined to turn what would often seem like misfortune or challenge into a teaching opportunity," I said.

"Sure seems like it," Pistis said, laughing.

"Life with him was never dull, that's for sure. He would always tell me to dream big. That in life people will often try to knock you down or tell you why you can't do something. He would then say, 'Do what they say can't be done, then show them how you did it.' I guess that is where I developed the desire to keep going when others would say something couldn't be done."

"Yeah, but look at all the different things you have done over the years," Pistis replied

"Yeah I guess that's true," I said.

"Tell me another lesson John taught you when you were young that was unusual." Pistis urged.

"Ok, this next story in a way is what taught me the importance of the power of visualization combined with practice, when it comes to developing new skill sets. Ever since I was five, I had this strong love for trucks. All I could think about were trucks. Semi-trucks, dump trucks … large and small I was mesmerized by them all. I remember asking John to take me to the local truck stop every chance I got so I could look at all the different trucks. On Friday afternoons we would go down to Miller Brewery, or out to the Waukesha Peterbilt dealership where there was a large parking lot that was always full of trucks. I would climb on them, and every now and then I could go inside of one. I even made a make-shift camera so I could take pictures of them.

I remember around age nine, I decided that I was going to write a book about the life of a trucker. I would go out to the 76 truck stop out on Ryan road and interview different truck drivers. Plus, the executive assistant at the Waukesha Peterbilt dealership would send me different brochures and magazines of different types of trucks for me to use as research. It's funny because those two places (the 76-truck stop and the Waukesha Peterbilt dealership) became icons for me. While friends went to the park and play, or play games at home, I would find a lot, any lot that was full of trucks. And I was in paradise. I would always say, 'Someday I'm going to drive one of these.'"

"Did you ever write the book?" Pistis asked.

"I finished the book, but it never went anywhere. Then, at some point during one of our moves, the book got lost. Who knows maybe someday I will write another one?

I remember around the time I was in second grade we had a Volkswagen bus. John made a panel with a clutch, brake, and gas pedal on it. In the middle of the board he welded a long pole with a steering wheel at the end that was on the passenger side floor of the bus and attached a long lever that was like a gear shifter so I could drive along with John. He then screwed a rope on to the ceiling of the bus that I could use as a chain for the air horn. There may not have been any noise when I pulled the chain, but to me it was just as cool.

Some say our minds can't tell the difference between reality and fantasy. All I know is that I learned how to listen to the noise of the engine and would often shift my lever just as John shifted the real one.

One weekend when I was around nine, we were visiting one of John's old friends, Maryann. She was complaining about a new car she just got and how it was really hard to learn how to shift it. John was telling her that it just takes practice.

"Oh yeah, easy for you to say," Maryann responded,

"I'm serious, John said laughing. It just takes a little practice. Even Sam has been practicing how to drive a manual transmission, I will bet you that Sam can drive it." "You're crazy! Sam's only nine and I can barely drive that car!" Maryann said laughing.

"If he can't, I will buy you dinner anywhere you want to go. But if he can, you have to make us a home cooked meal," He replied.

We had been traveling and eating at truck stops, so the sound of a home cooked meal sounded really nice. Laughing, she got up and said, "Ok follow me."

We walked out in front of her house as she threw me a set of keys to her light blue Volkswagen beetle and said, "Get into the driver's seat," as John jumped into the back seat and Maryann got into the passenger seat. Still in a state of shock over what was happening, I turned to look at Maryann and asked, "Are you sure?"

"Am I sure? Are you kidding? I know exactly where I want to go for dinner and it's not cheap. Besides, I will be surprised if you can even get the car into second gear," Maryann said, laughing. I thought to myself, 'I can't handle another restaurant no matter how good the food is. I really want her to make us a home cooked meal.'

Looking at the shift pattern, I noticed that it was the same as our Volkswagen bus, which I had memorized. Smiling, I started the car, put my seat belt on, looked at Maryann, and asked if she was ready.

"Show us what you've got kid, then let's go eat," She said laughing, while looking at John in the rear-view mirror.

"Ok then," I said as I pushed in the clutch, slid the shifter into reverse, and slowly backed out of the driveway. I then shifted into first and slowly let the clutch out, giving the car just the right amount of gas. The car moved forward as if it was on its own mission. I continued to give the car gas as we picked up speed. It was like listening to a full symphony.

The engine roared and the RPM's soared as I slid the transmission into second, then into third, and for a brief second into fourth. (The top gear at the time) As I approached the corner, slightly tapping on the brake, I quickly slid the transmission into third and let out the clutch as I slightly pushed on the brake. The RPM's revved up as the car slowed.

Easing off the break, I turned on the left turn signal, shifted down into second, and once again let out the clutch as I turned left back onto her street.

Victory was so close. Her house was only three driveways away. As I was down-shifting into first, she decided to freak out.

"Turn left! Turn left, you're going to miss the driveway!"

In an attempt to please her, I hit the brake and let out the clutch as the car slid into first. I cranked the steering wheel hard to the left. Down up down up, kaboom! She was right. Thanks to her yelling, I did miss the driveway. The car came to a stop right on top of a perfectly cut large tree stump that was just north of the driveway.

Turning the car off, as she sat there with a complete look of shock on her face, I got out and looked at the car. It was a perfect parking job except for the fact that the car was balancing on top of the giant tree stump. As I'm sure you're wondering, the bet was whether or not I could shift the car, not park it, so yes we did get a home-cooked meal once Maryann's shock wore off. Although, John did have to pay to have the car pulled off of the tree stump. And fortunately, there wasn't any damage done to the car, just my pride."

"Still, that's not bad driving for a nine-year-old," Pistis said chuckling.

"Thanks, it sure was a lot of fun," I answered.

"John was a great teacher. Another great adventure we went on was also when I was nine. Sue, a friend of John's, was moving from Milwaukee to San Diego once her two daughters were out of school. Knowing my love for trucks, and since John could drive a truck, she offered to give us two hundred dollars to drive their moving truck out to California. Then, we could use the money to fly back to Milwaukee. It sounded like a great trip, so he got my mom's permission to go and said, 'yes.'

It took us about five days to get there, as we stopped at many places along the way. We went to the Grand Canyon and several different museums. After we got the truck unloaded, we returned it to the rental company and went out for breakfast while we waited for Sue to pick us up. I sat there playing with these two toy trucks that I had, and John seemed to be in deep thought.

Sam / John hitchhiking

As I was finishing my pancakes, John looked at me and said,

'I was thinking; it's now the middle of June. We have $200 to fly back to Milwaukee with. We can go to the Airport tomorrow, get on a plane, and you will be back home tomorrow night. You will have the rest of your summer vacation to do whatever you want. Or, we could keep the $200, hitchhike home, and even make it a game.'

I sat there thinking to myself that I had never been on an airplane, so the idea of flying seemed kind of cool. But like John said, we would be home tomorrow night. Then what, what would I do for the rest of the summer. 'What do you mean by make it a game? How would hitchhiking home be a game?' I asked.

'Well, the game would be to hitchhike back to Milwaukee, which will most likely take a few weeks at best, and require many meals, and nights where we would need a place to stay. The challenge would be to see if we can make the trip across the country without spending very much money. Then the reward will be to take whatever money is left over and go out to eat every Friday night at any restaurant of your choice until the money runs out. What do you think?' John asked.

'Wow! Sounds like quite an adventure. And the idea of being able to eat out every Friday wherever I want sounds cool too. But to hitchhike all the way home; that's a long way. What if we can't get a ride?' I asked.

'Then we wait until someone comes along. Or we walk to wherever we can get a ride,' John answered.

'Well I do still have two and a half months left of summer vacation. And if we got home tomorrow, I'm not sure what I would do all summer,' I said.

'So, is it a plan then?' John asked.

'Yes, let's do it.' I replied.

Just then Sue walked into the diner. 'What are you two up to?' she asked.

'We decided to hitchhike back to Milwaukee!' I shouted, jumping up from my seat.

'You two decided what?' Sue asked with a curious look on her face.

'We decided to hitch hike back to Milwaukee,' I said again with a large smile.

'That's what I though you said. But why? You have plenty of money to fly back,' Sue asked.

'I'll tell you all about it on the way back to your house,' John said with a grin.

'Ok then, let's head home,' Sue said.

The next morning, we got up and packed our bags. Sue drove us to the edge of town, and the journey began," I told Pistis.

"Wow so how long did it take?" Pistis asked.

"Just over a month," I answered.

"Wow, sounds like quite a trip!"

"It was. There were many learning points along the way. I guess in a way, it's where I really developed patience and perseverance. There were days when we stood on the side of the road in 100+ degree temperatures all day waiting for a ride. Eventually, one always seemed to come, though."

"What were some of the different, more adventurous days like?" Pistis asked.

"One such adventure was when we tried to go to the Little America truck stop in Flagstaff, Arizona. We got dropped off at an intersection about 20 miles from the truck stop. We waited and waited, then finally decided to walk as we hitchhiked. Not always a good idea, because once you leave a major intersection, your chances of getting a ride go way down. As luck would have it, our chances of getting a ride seemed near impossible as we continued to walk. I remember my feet had blisters on them, and I was hungry and cold, so John put me on his shoulders and we kept walking. After what felt like forever, we finally turned the corner and there it was, Little America – the largest truck stop in the world.

We walked inside, sat down in the restaurant, and had dinner. After we finished dinner, we walked over to the Little America hotel where John said we might be able to spend the night. Except it cost fifty dollars a night to stay there. I sure was tired, but that was one-fourth of our allotted money. John asked me what I wanted to do, and I asked if there were any other places to sleep near there. The man behind the counter said that there was a small town only a couple of miles down the road that had many hotels there. So, we decided to head towards the town.

I remember it as if it was yesterday. We were walking down this dark lonely country road. The dark night sky was full of stars. You could hear what sounded like large dogs or coyotes howling off in the distance. Then all of a sudden, a car came driving at us, quickly turned into the lane near us, coming to a screeching halt, and the driver's door opened. John pushed me behind him and started to reach for a large hunting knife he had in a pocket in his large army coat. Just then red flashing lights on top of the car came on. I was never so glad to see a police car before.

The officer stepped out of his car and asked us what we were doing out there at 3:00 in the morning. John told him about our trip to Little America and how they said that there were hotels in the next town and that's where we were heading. I was so tired, the blisters on my feet were throbbing and I was becoming more scared as each moment passed. I broke down and started crying. The officer looked at me as asked what was wrong. Crying even harder now, I said that I was tired, hungry, and that all we wanted to do was find a place to sleep. The officer offered to drive us into town.

We went to a few different hotels and motels, but no one had any rooms available. The police officer said that there was a big convention in town and the next closet town was 25 miles away. He said that without a place to stay, we couldn't stay in town, but he could drive us to the edge of town and we could try our chances at the next town.

John said that if we could get to the edge of town, we could find a patch of trees to set up camp and try to get a ride to the next town in the morning. The officer looked at me, and said we were free to do whatever we wanted, however I looked like I really needed a good night sleep. He then suggested that we go with him back to the police station, and we could spend the night there. Then he would drive us to the end of town the next morning. John said, 'ok,' and I was happy we would have a place to stay but didn't really want to spend the night in jail either.

As it turned out, we got to the police station and they asked us a few more questions about what we were doing. The police station was small, with two jail cells in the back that the prisoners stayed in. Apparently, it was a quiet night because the only other person there besides us and the police officers was the town drunk - and he had the key to his own cell. They set two bunks up for us in the back of the station next to the cells and made us bacon and eggs for breakfast in the morning before driving us to the edge of town.

After saying our good-byes, we stood there for about an hour, then got picked up by a truck driver who drove us to Texas."

"Not many people can say they spent the night in jail, but as a guest," Pistis said, laughing.

"That is true, yeah in some ways the police station was like the one on the Andy Griffith Show."

"Where did you guys usually sleep at night?" Pistis asked.

"We would try to time it so we would get to a truck stop by the time it was late enough to sleep. They would many times have lounges that you could rest in, or they would have old abandoned trailers in the back of the truck stop that we would sleep in. If we couldn't find a truck stop, John would find a large bunch of trees where we could set up camp. And at least once a week we would stay in a hotel or motel so we could shower and really rest," I answered.

"Wow that sounds like quite an adventure."

"Yeah life with John was full of all sorts of adventures," I replied.

"Unfortunately, in the spring of my sixth-grade year, my mom and John decided they needed to go their separate directions and filed for a divorce. My mom and sister moved across town to a large gray tract house with my aunt and four other very dramatic

Sam stayed w/ John

women. At that time, John and I lived in a duplex that had a tenant on the first floor.

We stayed on the second floor; however, John also had a room in the basement that he stayed in most of the time. So, I might go a day or two without seeing him. During that time, when I felt lonely, I would think about the many stories I heard about Moses or Jesus and how they must have felt. I didn't know if they were true, but if they were, I know they would understand how I felt, and in a way, you could say they helped keep me company.

The following fall, I started seventh grade. About eight weeks into the school year, I couldn't take school anymore. The playground was like a war zone; fights broke out every day, and the teachers didn't seem to care. One afternoon on the playground, I was being pushed by another kid. As I was about to fight back, I found myself asking, 'What would Jesus do if He were in this situation?' I turned around, walked past my teacher, off the playground, and went home. John was the head chef at Marquette University. So, from that point forward, I would go to school in the morning, and as soon as they took attendance, I got on a bus and went to Marquette to help him in the kitchen.

Throughout the day, I listened to student workers talk about the different business and law classes they were taking. Over time, I became more and more interested in business and finances. When John didn't need my help, because the professors knew John, they would let me sit in on different business classes and workshops put on by the Small Business Administration. I was like a sponge, learning everything I could about business and finances, and swore that I would grow up and find a way to help small business owners design a solid financial foundation around their businesses and families.

I recalled stories I had heard about my grandparents; they had a wig shop that ended up going out of business. I listened to the teachers talk in the SBA classes about all sorts of business ideas and wondered if my grandparents had someone who could have helped them, they might have been able to save their wig shop. I looked at different small businesses around me, and they always seemed to be trying to do everything themselves. They were working very hard, yet one after another, these small businesses were failing. Then, later that year, John decided he was going to quit his job at Marquette and move to Hawaii with a girl who worked on the lunch line that he had been dating for a couple of months prior.

About three-fourths of the way through my seventh-grade year, I had to move in with my mom, sister, aunt, and the four other very dramatic women, who were devout feminists and would often sit around talking about how awful men were. (Not an environment a 12-year-old boy should ever have to deal with.) I didn't know which was worse; being by myself or having to listen to them rant and rave. So, I would come home from school and go straight to my room. My life felt like it was turned upside down.

I kept to myself most of the time and couldn't stop thinking about all the lessons I had learned in the SBA classes at Marquette University. I started working with modeling clay, and built a huge city out of modeling clay, incorporating many of the things I had learned that later became the foundation for a powerful business plan I have been working on ever since."

"Wow, what a way to turn what must have been a very confusing time in your life into a great learning time. What a great learning experience for someone so young," Pistis replied.

"I know, I guess that's why it hurt so much when John decided to move to Hawaii. I lost a great friend, teacher, and in many ways a great father. That was probably around the time that I really started to question my faith," I said.

"Question your faith? You were in seventh grade when he left. Most seventh graders question whether or not they should go out for the basketball team, or if they should ask the girl sitting in front of them to the movies, not their faith," Pistis said, chuckling. "For me, the sense of faith that I had and the sense that my silent mentor was often nearby, was often the only true thing I had that always remained stable, no matter what was going on around me," I replied.

"Ok, so what do you think was the turning point for you? You had just lost John from your life. You were living in an environment that didn't sound very fun, and your faith was rocky at best," Pistis said.

"In all honesty, I think it was my time at Holy Rosary. Sister Ellen was a huge influence on me," I answered.

"Your time at Holy Rosary?"

"As it turned out, I had to go back to school. Because there were only two months left of the school year, I couldn't go to the neighborhood school, and was told that I had to return to the school I used to attend.

I couldn't believe it. Once again, I was being thrown into a situation where I would have to fight to survive. Everything inside me resisted going back to that school. And if I did, I didn't think I would live to talk about it.

Monday morning came. I got up, left the house, and was on my way back to my old school. I walked towards the bus stop, started to shake, and then started to cry. I didn't know what to do. I didn't want to go back to that school and I didn't want to go home. I had so many questions, and knew I needed answers.

Instead of getting on the bus and going to school, I turned right and walked around the corner. As I stared ahead in amazement, I saw a cross on the front of a school. On the wall next to it were two words: Holy Rosary. Still shaking, I walked into the school and asked a kid who was standing by the door where the principal's office was. I walked down a long hall and into a dimly lit corner office. Sitting in front of me was a thin, gray-haired lady looking at a book. On the desk in front of her was a silver and black name plate that read Sister Ellen.

She looked up, and asked, 'Can I help you, young man?' With a slight crack in my voice, I said "I don't know, but I hope so. I would like to go to school here.'

Looking around, she asked, "Where are your parents?"

'They are at work,' I answered.

'Do you mean you want to go to school here next year?' she asked.

'No, Ma'am. I mean today,' I said, trying to keep from crying.

'It's not that simple. Your parents have to fill out an application to register you. Then, if you're accepted, they have to pay tuition,' she explained.

Tears started to roll down my face. Trying to keep my voice from cracking, I confessed, 'My mom doesn't have any money. Plus she doesn't believe in God, so she would never sign me up. I won't go back to my old school. I haven't been to school for six months. I have nowhere else to go. When I saw the cross above the door, I knew this is where I needed to be.' I then told her my story.

Sister Ellen sat there thinking for what seemed like forever. She then asked what my mom's name was and where she worked. Making some notes, she got up and asked me to follow her. We walked into a classroom, where she introduced me to the teacher and told me to take a seat.

Later, I found out that Sister Ellen went back to her office, called my mom at work, told her that I had walked into the school, and what I said. She then told my mom that if she would give her approval and come to the school to fill out the necessary paperwork, they would allow me to finish out the school year there. Sister Ellen said she would also arrange to have the tuition taken care of so my mom would not have to be burdened by it.

I finished out the school year at Holy Rosary, and Sister Ellen told me that I was welcome to come back the next year.

However, I would have to redo seventh grade, because I had missed so much school that my schoolwork was still on a seventh-grade level. I was in shock. For the first time in years, I had made friends with my classmates and the thought of coming back a grade below them was inconceivable.

Sister Ellen listened to my concerns. I really wanted to, no I *needed* to stay with my new friends. Sister Ellen said that she understood, but that even if she allowed me to move up into eighth grade, if my schoolwork wasn't at a ninth-grade level by the end of the year, she wouldn't be able to let me to graduate.

After a couple of moments of silence, I said, 'Sister Ellen, I understand that I fell behind and that I need to catch up to the rest of my class. I also know that if I work really hard, I can do that. If I'm going to repeat the school year, I would rather do so, knowing that at least I tried my best first.' I then made her a proposition, 'If I do all the eighth-grade work during the day and all the seventh-grade work at night so that I'm at a 9th grade level by the end of the year, would you allow me to come back with my classmates as an eighth grader next year?'

With a smile on her face, Sister Ellen told me that my idea seemed reasonable, but if I didn't get caught up I would have to redo eighth grade again."

"Let me guess, you finished all the work," Pistis said smiling.

"Yes, you guessed it. I did all the work and graduated with my eighth-grade class. As it turns out, I am still friends with some of my classmates today. That year, Sister Ellen also helped answer many of the questions I had about life. She lit a light that has burned brightly for many years since. At graduation, I thanked Sister Ellen for believing in me and for giving me a chance. I told her that one day I would build an organization that would help improve the lives of hundreds, if not thousands of people. And, I would make sure people knew she had helped make it happen.

Smiling, she gave me a big hug, and said, 'I believe you will, Sam. Just keep following your dream, and amazing things will happen for you.' Unfortunately, that was the last time I saw Sister Ellen. Whenever I hear people say, 'There's no God.' I think to myself, 'If they only knew Sister Ellen, they wouldn't say that.'"

"Wow that's a great example of the Holy Spirit at work. Was that the turning point in your faith?"

"Yeah I guess in many ways it was. But that's what's so strange. Even though everyone around me were devout atheists, and put religion down whenever they could, I had a deep inner sense of faith that God was always by my side.

During my freshmen year of high school, I ended up going to a college preparatory school. Life was really starting to look up. The high school only had around 200 kids in it, so everyone knew each other. I was really into disco and became really good at dancing, so I quickly became one of the most popular kids there.

I started dating a really sweet girl named Karen. We quickly became very close. It seemed like we spent every waking hour together. When we were together it was as if time came to a standstill. I really liked her and would even find myself daydreaming about marrying her. Karen and I started attending a Baptist church in Brown Deer on the northwest side of Milwaukee near her house. We joined the choir, and even though I often felt like a square peg in a round hole, I loved going to the church and loved being in the choir. Life was great!"

"It sounds like things were really starting to work out for you," Pistis said with a large smile.

"Yeah, it sure seemed like it. I remember one day, we had choir practice. It was a very important practice before a big church concert, and the church van broke down. At first, they were going to cancel choir practice. Everyone was upset because we really needed the practice. So, at the last minute, I offered to pick everyone up and bring them to practice. The choir director was really happy and said that if I could do that, it would be great. That way we wouldn't have to cancel choir.

'Anything to make sure we are ready for this weekend,' I said to the choir director, smiling.

I borrowed my sister's car, drove to Brown Dear about ten miles from her house, and proceeded to pick all the students up. As I dropped off the last group of kids, Pastor Jim came up to me.

'Thank you so much Sam for picking up all the kids and bring them to choir practice. But I have to ask you; aren't you only 15?' He said with a concerned look on his face.

'Yes, I am why do you ask?'

'Because, if I'm not mistaken, don't you need to be 16 to get a driver's license?' Pastor Jim asked.

Mentoring That Makes Cents

'Yes, but I'm on a mission for God. It seems to me that God is above man's laws.'

'Yes and no,' Pastor Jim responded, 'God's laws rule above all else, but in the end, because we are all people of earth, we still need to abide by the rules of mankind unless they go against all that is holy. And, unfortunately the threat of cancelling choir practice, as much practice as you all may need, doesn't constitute a true need to break the law, even in God's name. So, it's best that you leave the car here, and I will find a way to take everyone home once practice is over. And that includes you,' Pastor Jim said laughing.

We had a great practice. Once it was over, Pastor Jim and a few of the elders took everyone home. The next day, I came back with my sister and got her car. The next weekend, we had an amazing concert. Many said it was the best concert they had ever heard in that church.

If I only knew what was about to come; life was going so well! I was the most popular kid in school, which for a freshman was pretty cool. I was part of a great church, I really liked Karen, and my faith in God and Jesus Christ was really growing strong. However, another turning point in my life was about to begin.

Over the summer, between my ninth and tenth grade year, my mom found out that we had to move. At that point, my father was living in Waukesha, so she thought that it might be a good idea for me to live with my father for a while.

I was stunned; life as I knew it was over. Within three weeks I had moved from the east side of Milwaukee and was living in Waukesha. No more Brown Deer Baptist Church. No more choir. No more being the cool kid in school. I was now a poor city kid stuck in the middle of a bunch of rich suburban kids who thought they were cool and had the money to back it up. Then, as if things weren't bad enough, I called Karen to tell her about the new school. She told me that she never wanted to talk to me again. (I found out later on that my dad told Karen's mother that I really liked a girl in my new school, and that her daughter shouldn't call me anymore.)

I couldn't believe it; my whole life was turned upside down. I couldn't understand how God could give me so much, and then take it all away. First, I was angry. I started to think that maybe my mom was right. Maybe there really wasn't a God? How could there be? Life was what it was. It was a dog eat dog world, and we were stuck with what life gave us. It was the first time since I was nine, when I would sit in my room by myself and wonder if my stepfather was in the basement, that I felt truly alone. I broke down and cried.

The next day, I got up and went to the new school. I felt angry and alone. I didn't want to talk to anyone. I just wanted to be left alone. I kept wondering what happened to my best friend, my silent mentor? Why was I shutting him out? In the past, no matter how bad things would get, I could always feel His presence. Yet at that point, I felt empty and alone.

I walked into the school, started to go towards my locker, and accidentally bumped into a guy standing there. He called me a name, and one of his friends grabbed me from behind. The guy I bumped into took a swing at me. It seemed as if everything froze. I remember flipping the guy behind me over my shoulder stopping the guy in front of me from hitting me. I turned and with a side kick, sent the guy who swung at me, into a locker. Then I turned around as tears began to run down my face and left the school.

I walked into downtown Waukesha, got on a Greyhound bus, and went back to Milwaukee. During the ride to Milwaukee, I sat there staring out the window wondering why God was doing this to me. Was I really alone? Had I been just fooling myself before? I kept thinking to myself, was my mom right after all? Yet, I knew in my heart that she couldn't be. I started to think about how Sister Allen would say, 'Follow your heart, and God will always be by your side.'

I thought about all the challenges Jesus had to overcome, yet He always moved forward with His mission. And as He had his Father by His side, I had Him. Ever since I was little, God had never left my side, so who was I to second guess Him now? I had no idea what was to come, but I once again finally started to feel His presence, and knew I wasn't alone.

Later that day, my father called my mom and told her that I had been kicked out of the high school for fighting, that the kid I sent into a locker broke his arm, and that I should come pick up my things and move back in with her. However, she didn't have any room, so I was once again stuck in between houses. Fortunately, a friend of hers had a spare room and I was able to stay there for a while.

By now it was mid-October, and Brown Deer Baptist Church was having a fall weekend retreat. I was invited to attend the retreat and it sounded like it would be fun. Plus, I knew that Karen and her mom would be there, so maybe I would be able to win her back. Friday night and most of Saturday flew by. As we were getting ready for dinner, Pastor Jim and I were talking about the move, and he asked me if I would give my testimony at the bonfire that evening. I really respected the pastor but smiled and said, 'Yeah right, me. What do I have to say to anyone one here? I'm just a punk kid. There are a lot of people here who know the Bible a lot better than I do.'

'You don't have to quote the bible,' he said, smiling.

'I don't like talking in front of people. Besides, I wouldn't know what to say.'

'We will sing a few songs, I will give a short message, and you would come up and give your testimony. Then, as we close, I always invite people to come forward, if they would like to invite Jesus into their lives.'

'I don't know, I appreciate you asking me. But if Jesus wanted me to be his witness, he would have left me at your church, where I was in choir and wouldn't have turned my life upside down. No one would take me seriously anyway.'

'Go for a walk and pray about it. If you change your mind, let me know. But you have to believe in your heart that if you decide to do it, God will be by your side.'

'Ok,' I said and walked off. After walking around for a while, I couldn't help thinking that if the pastor wanted me to give a testimony, who was I to question his trust and God's power? So, I went back and told him I would do it.

That night the weather was beautiful. We all sat around a large campfire, sang songs, and the pastor gave a short message until it was my turn. First, fear set in as I stood up and walked around to where the pastor was standing. My voice started to quiver and I could feel my knees start to shake. As I walked, I looked across the campfire at Karen and her mother who had not yet talked to me since the night my dad called. I could feel tears running down my cheeks. Then I heard the words, as if someone were standing right behind me, 'I am with you, I always have been with you. Just tell your story as I direct you.' My voice cleared, I stopped shaking, and the tears dried. I gave my testimony.

'I am here tonight to talk about my best friend. A man who, when I was alone, sat at my side and when I was afraid, gave me strength. A man who, when I would hear someone say, 'You shouldn't have been born, you were a mistake.' would say, 'I don't make mistakes; you are here to bring more light to the world.' A man who, when someone would say, 'You're just a punk kid.' would say, 'You are here to do great things.' A man who never said, 'I don't know how.' or 'I can't.' but instead said, 'Follow me and I will show you the way.' A man who lived his life unsurpassed by any other. A man who gave his life, so that we can have everlasting life. That man, my best friend, my mentor, my Lord, is Jesus Christ.

Growing up I always heard people say God is this, or God isn't that. There are many unanswered questions I have about God. But I do know this: throughout my life, the world has let me down over and over again, but Jesus has never left my side. Even when I shut him out, He was always there with me. I could give far more examples of how he has been at work in my life than I have time for.'

I stood there in front of everyone in complete surprise as almost everyone including the Pastor, Karen and her mom, sat there with tears rolling down their cheeks. With tears starting to roll down

43

my own cheeks, I then said, 'I don't know why I'm here in front of you now, I'm far from perfect.

All I ever wanted was to live my life as close to the way Jesus had lived. I would often ask, 'If Jesus was here, what would He do?' I don't know why life has been so crazy at times, but I do know this: as long as I have Jesus by my side, I will never be alone. So, if anyone here is feeling alone, please let Jesus into your life. He is here for you, but you have to allow Him in.'

The Pastor came up and stood next to me as he gave the closing prayer and said, 'If there is anyone who would like to invite Jesus into their lives, please stand up and come forward.'
I stood there in complete amazement as I watched 15 people come up and invite Jesus in their lives that night.

The retreat came to an end. We all went back home, and life went back to being a crazy roller coaster ride. To this day, even though I have not set foot back inside of Brown Deer Baptist Church, I have never been the same.

Then, as the summer was coming to an end, my dad called out of the blue and asked if I wanted to go to church with my stepmother and him, then go out for lunch after. At first, I wasn't sure what to think. I was still really angry at him but going seemed like the right thing to do. So, I went. I still remember that morning as if it were yesterday. My dad was attending a large church called Elmbrook that was near his house, and Stuart Briscoe, the senior pastor at the time, gave a message on God's grace.

I remember sitting there as he talked, thinking to myself, 'If God truly is a graceful God, then who was I to question His direction for my life?' Sure, I may not like the current conditions, and didn't understand why He kept turning my life upside down. However, ever since I gave my testimony at the church camp, it was obvious that I was being prepared or primed for something great. That day I devoted my life to serving God and becoming a great disciple of Christ.

I knew that wherever I was, whatever I was doing, Jesus was always at work within me. I would get calls from people, often people I never met, with problems that I would have to help them solve. One such example was a call I received at 3:00am from a girl who was crying, which turned out to be a wrong number. After talking to the girl on the phone for two hours, I found out she was pregnant and believed that her father wouldn't want anything to do with her.

She kept saying that she had to run away because if her father found out she was pregnant he would kill her. She was scared, didn't have any money, and was only sixteen. I told her that I wanted her home phone number and her father's name so if anything did happen to her, I would be her witness. I told her that her father might get very angry, but he wouldn't kill her because she was still his little girl. And if she ever believed her life was in danger, I knew who she was.

She said she would go home and talk to her mother and father, and we hung up. I went back to bed. I learned a few years later that as it turned out, she went home and after a lot of contemplation, her parents decided to adopt her baby and she finished school."

"Wow, that's a great example of how Christ works through us if we let Him," Pistis said.

"Yeah, that's for sure!" I replied.

"The important thing to remember is that while trusting in God to lead you, it is important that you stay in contact with Him. God still yearns for a relationship with you. As you honor Him in prayer, he will guide you according to that prayer.

Earlier, you said that at times you felt like you only wanted to be left alone and like your life kept being turned upside down. Because of that, your faith was continually being tested. You referred a couple of times to how you would question if your mom was really right, that there was no such thing as God. What did you mean by that?" Pistis asked.

Just then the plane hit a pocket of rough air. I tensed up as the turbulence made the plane bounce around, Pistis smiled and said, "Relax Sam, just envision God's hand being under this plane."

Surprised at what Pistis just said, because that was the same prayer I always say when I'm on a plane and it's about to take off, I replied, "I just really hate flying."

Just then the pilot came over the intercom and announced that we were climbing to a higher altitude and the turbulence should smooth out soon. "There is always something calming about the captain letting us know that he has control of the aircraft," I told Pistis.

He who loses money, loses much; He who loses a friend loses much more; He who loses faith, loses all – Eleanor Roosevelt

Not so, but we also glory in our sufferings, because we know that sufferings produce perseverance: Perseverance, charter or hope. And hope does not put us to shame, because God's love has been poured out into our hearts through the Holy Spirit, who has been given to us.
Romans 5:3-5

CHAPTER 3

A Crisis of Faith

The plane finally smoothed out and I could feel myself starting to relax again. The flight attendant came by with a basket of treats and asked Pistis and me if we wanted anything. I took a bag of potato chips and a cookie, and Pistis took a cookie and a banana.

I thought about the question Pistis just asked me about why at times I felt like I only wanted to be left alone, how it felt like my life kept being turned upside down, and because of that, my faith was continually being tested so I would question if my mom was really right; that there was no such thing as God.

I paused, took a bite of my cookie, repeated his question and continued, "What did I mean by what I was saying? Well I guess as I continued to get older, I often wondered why, if there really was a God, he allowed my life to seem so out of control? Then, He would bring someone into my life who had it far worse than I could have imagined, and I would find myself having to help that person."

"Like the pregnant girl," Pistis said with a smile.

"Exactly. Or like another time, I got fired from a restaurant job because the owner found out that I had dropped out of high school. But then the owner called me three weeks later, after finding out that his son had also dropped out of high school and asked me if I would try to convince him to go back to school. The crazy thing was that someone who knew both me and the owner told the owner that I was his best hope for getting his son to go back to school."

"Did you say you would talk to his son, or tell the owner to jump in a lake?" Pistis asked, laughing.

"I told him to have his son meet me at the restaurant and that I would talk to him."

"Wow, what did you say to the son?"

"I asked him why he dropped out of school.

He replied by saying that he was sick of school and that he didn't want to go anymore.

I asked him if he loved his dad and told him that school was very important to him, so important that he fired me as soon as he found out that I too had dropped out of school. He then said that he hated school. So I had him follow me into the kitchen and told him that if he didn't finish school, his dad would likely cut him off and that he would likely end up washing dishes for a living. But, if he finished school, his dad would probably give him the restaurant someday. I then told him I would give anything to be in his shoes, and the fact that he was so willing to just throw it all away made me sick. I then turned around and left the restaurant.

I found out a week later that he went back to school and told his dad he was sorry for upsetting him so much."

"Wow, did you get your job back?" Pistis said, giggling.

"Nope, but it never was about me. I figured God put me in that restaurant so I would be able to help the owner's son. In the end, I didn't feel like I could depend on anything or anyone to be in my life for very long. So, I always tried to keep a strong connection to my faith. If I ever started to feel alone or challenged by something, I would often repeat the words, 'I know that through Christ anything is possible." I always tried to stay true to that faith for myself, but also so I could be a good example for those around me.'"

Smiling, Pistis then said, "He who did not spare his own son, but delivered Him up for us all, will also freely give me all things. Romans 8:32. Or another one of my favorites, God has given me all things that pertain to life and godliness, through the knowledge of Him who has called me to glory and virtue. 2 Peter 1:3."

"I sure hope so. I just want to be a good and faithful servant. I can't help thinking about all the things that people said were impossible, yet somehow, some way, someone was able to make the impossible possible. Take flying for example. We're sitting here on a Boeing 737 looking out over a mountain from 30,000 feet above. Yet, people laughed at the Wright brothers as they attempted to create the first airplane. Thank goodness they didn't listen to the naysayers and give up. This trip is long enough without having to drive all the way from Milwaukee, Wisconsin to Seattle, Washington. Then again, if Ford would have listened to those who called him stupid and never completed the automobile assembly line, we could be taking a horse to Seattle. Granted, I feel for the horse and buggy manufactures as they watched their industry fall by the wayside. But then again, without future advancement, we would miss out on the many blessings that life has to offer," I said.

"Very true, it's so important that people dare to dream, reach for the stars, keep the faith that all dreams are possible, and take ownership of their dreams. People are created for greatness, but it's up to them to make their dreams become reality. Sure, others might say it's not possible, or it's never been done before. I say, 'Go for it anyway.' First, they need to see it as if it's already completed, then the second step is to create the plan, or blueprint, showing the steps necessary to make it become reality. Then put it to prayer. Take Walt Disney for example; he saw Disney World as a completed theme park way before it ever became reality.

Reality must first start with an idea of the way something should or could be. Then through faith and prayer, the process of it becoming reality becomes more and more possible. Take the creation of life as an example. Many call the birth of a newborn baby a miracle; I would be more inclined to say it's God's divine glory manifested in life form," Pistis said, smiling.

"Good point. I remember one day after our daughter Sabrina was born, Jennifer said that she wanted our next kids to be twins. She really wanted to have three kids but didn't want to go through the pain of childbirth three times if she could help it. Not only that, she went on to say that she wanted to have a boy with straight hair and a girl with curly hair. That way I would have a son and Sabrina would have a little sister. Smiling, I looked at Jennifer and asked if she wanted anything else?

'Well, I hope that they will take care of each other and are healthy of course,' she replied."

"Well, you have to admit that what she was hoping for seemed reasonable," Pistis said, chuckling.

"That's true. But I still couldn't help being worried because we don't have twins in our immediate family. So even though it sounded nice, it would almost take a miracle for it to happen. Jennifer was a young Christian, and yes, I believed in the power of prayer, but I didn't want her to be disappointed. I don't remember reading anywhere that God takes special orders when it comes to making babies. Yet, I was really proud of how her faith was growing stronger each day."

"One should never underestimate the power of the Lord," Pistis said, smiling.

"You do make a good point. Almost two years had gone by since Jennifer told me about having twins. We were busy as ever trying to keep up with Sabrina, then just about a year-and-a-half old. Between Jennifer's new responsibilities in her job, my trying to grow Newcastle Limousine, a business I had started after Sabrina was born, and all the other things going on in our lives; it seemed like there was never enough time or energy for intimacy. Then, one night after returning home from a conference, we went out for a romantic dinner, went home, put Sabrina to bed, and for the first time since Sabrina was born, magic happened.

About four weeks later Jennifer started to show the signs of being pregnant. But how could it be? One magical night is hardly the recipe for pregnancy. After all, Jennifer was still breastfeeding Sabrina. Little did I know that night was to become even more magical then I had thought. Jennifer was indeed pregnant. So, over the course of the next few weeks, we began a series of tests to make sure everything was ok with the baby.

Friday, May 30th, 1997, the start of Memorial Day weekend at 5:00pm, we received a message from Jennifer's doctor's nurse saying they got the results back from the blood test she had done earlier in the week. The message went as follows,

'Hi Jennifer, this is Nurse Jackie from Dr. Green's office. We got the results back from your blood test showing the health of your baby's brain function. It's extremely important that you call our office first thing Tuesday morning, as we are closed for Memorial Day weekend and schedule an ultrasound because the test results were way off and we need to make sure the baby's brain function is okay.'

I grabbed the phone and tried to call her back, but they were already closed for the weekend. We were in shock. How could that happen? Why would anybody leave a message like that? Jennifer and I just stared at each other in complete shock. To make things worse, we were supposed to go away with some friends for the weekend.

We cancelled our plans with our friends and took Sabrina to the beach so we could think. I spent the better part of Saturday reading and researching all the different things that could go wrong causing the blood test to be off. True, Jennifer was pregnant which was great. But could we handle a baby with challenges? Sabrina was still so young. Granted many people have similar challenges or worse and they persevere through them. But could we? Neither of us knew the answer to that. We spent the better part of Saturday talking and praying about what to do."

"Wow, it sounds like it was a true test of faith for both Jennifer and you."

"That's for sure. The crazy thing is just one week before, Jennifer was telling a friend from church about how she was praying for twins. The idea of having twins already made me nervous; after all we already had a small child. And, the fact that she was praying with such detail still seemed strange to me. It was almost like she was placing a cosmic shopping order. Who were we to feel like we were entitled to such grace? Now, I just prayed that our baby would be healthy. And, if not, that we would be given the strength to properly handle what was to come. It became a weekend of true inner reflection.

Tuesday morning came. We got up and took Sabrina to the babysitter's house, then headed to the hospital where the ultrasound was being performed. As we talked about the potential outcome, so many questions came up. Do we keep the baby if there was something seriously wrong with it? We still had time if we decided not to. But then what would we tell Sabrina? Would we be able to find help? We barely knew how to take care of Sabrina. Do we put the baby up for adoption? Maybe there was a family out there that was better equipped to handle such a challenge.

I pulled over as tears started to run down my cheeks. Many different emotions surfaced. Why God? What did I do wrong? I moved across the world per your request. I married Jennifer and brought her back to the United States. I shared your stories and glory with her. I told her about the importance of prayer. How could you do this to her? She didn't ask for this! She followed me and believed me when I told her about your glory. Why? Why? I truly don't get it. And why did she listen to me? Who was I? I was just a punk kid from the 'hood who decided to move across the world.

Just then, the words jumped out at me as if they were on fast forward. 'Who are you? You are my son. You have always been so faithful. Why now the sudden loss of faith? I have never left your side. Stay faithful, no matter what the outcome! I will empower you to overcome any challenges put before you.' I just sat there in complete silence.

'Are you ok?' Jennifer asked me softly.

'Yeah, I'm fine. I am sorry. I don't know what happened. I'm just so scared.'

'I know. I am too,' she replied.

'Sam, remember what you said to me when we were still in Taiwan? That we needed to stay faithful, that through God's grace all things are possible?'

'Yeah, I guess.'

Then this sense of calmness came over us. We both came to the decision that Jennifer was still carrying our baby inside of her. That we had to stay strong no matter what the outcome. We needed to have faith that we would be given the necessary strength to handle what was to come. I quickly pulled away from the curb and headed towards the hospital."

"Yet another great example of true inner faith," Pistis replied, with a large smile.

"I don't know if I was mad, scared, or just plain hopeful, but who was I to second-guess God's power or ultimate reasoning? We pulled into the hospital parking lot, got out of the car, and walked hand-in-hand into the clinic. As we entered the building and walked into the waiting area, a medium-sized thin brown-haired lady asked us if she could help us.

'I hope so,' I said, 'We have an appointment to get an ultrasound done.'

'Ok, please follow me,' the receptionist said.

She had Jennifer change into a hospital gown and lie down on an adjustable bed; and had me sit in a chair next to her. Shortly thereafter, the technician entered the room smiling and said, 'Hi I'm Sarah. I'm going to be doing the ultrasound today. Now it may feel a bit cold but rest assured, it won't hurt. Before we get started, do you have any questions?' she asked.

'Nope not yet,' we answered.

'Ok then let's get started,' she replied. Sarah hooked the machine up to Jennifer. After spreading a strange grease onto Jennifer's stomach, Sarah slid a paddle around listening for different sounds and trying to get a picture of what was going on.

I was sitting there trying to look calm but was terrified underneath. What was wrong with our sweet little baby? Was it going to be ok? Were we going to be ok? Thought after thought raced through my mind.

At first, nothing; you could have heard a pin drop. A slight look of worry flowed across Sarah's face. Then there is was. Bum bump, bum bump, bum bump. The look of worry quickly left, as Sarah's face lit up with a big smile. 'Of course the brain's function or chemicals are way off the chart. There are two of them.'

'What do you mean there are two of them? Like the baby has two heads?' I asked.

'No silly, there are two babies.'

'What twins? No way! Really? Twins? But how?'

'Really! How?' Sarah replied smiling.

'And now you're going to tell me it's a boy and a girl, right?' I asked with a puzzled look on my face.

'Well it's a little early to tell, but it's possible,' Sarah replied.

My eyes swelled up with tears as I looked at Jennifer. 'Everything is going to be all right. You did it. God answered your prayers. We are going to have twins.' I said.

'I know Mike. All that worry was for nothing.' Jennifer replied.

'Well now at least we are prepared for anything,' I said.

'So, you two *wanted* twins?' Sarah asked.

'Wanted twins?! Jennifer has been praying for twins for the last two years. I told her not to get her hopes up, because twins don't run in our immediate family. But every night she prayed none-the-less. Not only that, she prayed and asked for a boy with straight hair and a girl with curly hair. I would tell her I didn't think God took requests for such things, but she still prayed her prayer none-the-less."

'Wow that's an amazing story,' Sarah said smiling, as she packed up her stuff and gave us some paperwork.

'Ok, I will need you two to come back in two weeks for another ultrasound just to make sure everything is alright. Although after what you just said, it looks like you're in good hands. I don't think you have too much to worry about!' Sarah said, with a large smile on her face."

"That sure is an amazing story of how God can work miracles in our lives, if we will just believe in Him," Pistis replied.

"The crazy thing is Jennifer's whole pregnancy was a series of miracles leading up to the day Monica and Sam were born.

One morning about seven-and-a-half months into the pregnancy, Jennifer and I had her weekly doctor's appointment scheduled for 11:00am. I got to her office at 10:30am to pick her up, and she said that her stomach really hurt. So, I told her that we could see if the doctor could give her something to relax her stomach. We then headed to the clinic for our appointment.

As we walked into the clinic for our appointment, the receptionist looked up from her desk, saw it was us, and said that she was really sorry, but Dr. Green got caught up at the hospital so we would have to go over there for our appointment.

'Seriously!' I said, 'That's six blocks away and my wife has a bad stomachache. Now we have to go over there.'

'I'm sorry,' The receptionist said again, 'but that's the only way to see the doctor.'

'Ok then, we will go over to the hospital.'

'Sorry again, I'll tell Dr. Green you're on your way.'

We got to the hospital and checked in, and a few minutes later Dr. Green walked into the room. She too apologized for us having to come over to the hospital and asked how everything was going.

'It's going well, except that I have really bad cramps. Is there something you can give me for the pain?' Jennifer asked.

'Probably, let's see after I examine you a little more,' Dr Green replied.

'Ok.'

Dr. Green poked and prodded, and as she finished the examination, she looked up and said,

'Well, I have good news and not so good news. The good news is that in about 30 minutes your stomachache should be gone. The not so good news is that you will have two babies to take its place. You are in full labor; the reason for the bad cramps is that the babies are breach causing them not to be able to move.'

'Really? I'm in labor?!' Jennifer asked with a strange look on her face.

'But she's not due for another six weeks,' I said.

'I know, but with twins they can come early. That's why we have you come in for an exam every week.' Dr. Green then called out a bunch of orders and people came running into the room. They wheeled Jennifer into another room as I followed. Within 30 minutes the C-section was complete, and Monica and Sammy were born.

As the doctor started to close Jennifer up, another nurse was cleaning Monica and Sammy, and then weighed them. The challenge with premature babies is that their lungs and other internal organs may not be fully developed. So, they may have to stay in an incubator until they become fully developed.

Amazingly, Sammy tested 95% in all the categories and Monica tested 98% so they only had to spend four days in the special baby ward.

It was 3:00pm, and Jennifer was resting in her room and Sammy and Monica were there next to her. Dr. Green entered the room and asked how we were doing.

'I'm tired but you were right, my cramps are gone,' Jennifer said as she looked up and smiled.

'That's good,' Dr Green replied. 'I must say though, you two must have a guardian angel looking out for you.'

'Why do you say that?' I asked.

'Because, even though twins can come early; it's unusual for them to be this early, and breach in the way that they were. If you weren't here in the hospital this morning, Jennifer's labor would have continued to get worse and the twins would have caused severe pain if not worse. Chances are you would have ended up calling 911 and having to rush to the hospital. Let's just say things could have gone horribly wrong very quickly,' Dr. Green said.

'Wow! I know this whole pregnancy has been amazing. First, with them being twins, and then being a boy and a girl. The only thing left is for Sam to have straight hair while Monica has curly hair,' I said laughing while looking at Jennifer.

'Yep, you guessed it. Sam has straight hair and Monica has curly hair. It feels like only yesterday. But just last month they went off to college," I said to Pistis with a big smile on my face.

"I thought when you first said Jennifer wanted twins after already having a small child at home, that you were pushing the outer limits, but that's a whole series of miracles, and a great story," Pistis said, laughing.

The flight attendant approached and handed Pistis and me another bottle of water. Thanking the flight attendant, I drank the water she had just handed me, and continued by saying, "The hardest part was that it seemed like the challenges kept coming one after another. I just wanted to live a normal life.

My biggest struggle is that even though I know that all things will work out, I need to stay patient and have faith. Lord knows I have enough reasons to believe, yet I still find myself on my knees totally frustrated just as God opens the next door, often with the previous door slamming shut behind me."

"Yes, that is often the case, and sometimes that's when you are the most coachable. It's important that you always remember this equation: Faith + Patience = God's divine glory," Pistis replied. He then went on to say, "As it's written in Mark 11:24 'Therefore I tell you, whatever you ask for in prayer, believe that you have received it, and it will be yours.'

It's OK to be doubtful and question certain teachings. It's wise to be skeptical. And, it's natural to ask why, but don't get so caught up in trying to figure out why that you forget to solve for how. And sometimes the how is having the faith and the patience to allow God's divine glory to truly shine," Pistis said.

"Very true, I remember one particular day back when we were living in Seattle and the kids were still really young, as if it were yesterday. One morning, Jennifer and I got into a heated argument and she left for work, still angry. I left her an angry note venting my frustrations and left on a twelve-hour drive to help my mom with something. By the time I returned home, it was around 3:00AM. Jennifer was sound asleep. She had also left me a note venting her frustrations, except that *her* note ended with 'Maybe we should get a divorce'.

What? The D word? I couldn't believe it! I walked into the living room and dropped to my knees. I looked up at the ceiling in utter despair, tears running down my cheeks, and screamed, 'Why God!? Why? You told me I needed to leave my home and leave everything that mattered to me and you would show me the way. You told me to go to Taiwan with only one hundred dollars and a one-way ticket. Even though everyone told me I was crazy and if I went, that I probably would die over there; I went anyway. Whatever you asked of me I tried to do. I know you are here with me guiding me, yet I feel so alone, Why God!? Why?'

Totally overrun by emotion, my body trembling, tears streaming down my cheeks, I cried out again, 'Why God!? Why? Why can't I be like everyone else? I don't want very much; never did. I don't need very much; just a simple loving family. I'm here for you Lord, you know that! Tell me what you want to do, and I will do it. But why do you keep sending me on these journeys only to fail and not tell me why? Why God!? Why?'

Once again, as if someone was standing behind me, a loud voice rang out, 'Stop asking why, and start asking how! You know why. I've shown you why! It's time that you started asking how.' Wiping the tears from my eyes, I called out 'What do you mean how?' It was at that point I knew it was time to pull all my lessons together and start working on the how. How was I going to hold true to God's purpose for me and not what I thought others expected from me?"

Nodding, Pistis said, "It sounds to me that God's purpose for you is to share those stories with people; to become the leader that God has been preparing you to become. There are many different stories and opinions about God's existence and His always-present guidance in our lives. Some people equate this to the law of attraction or a universal law, others to a far more spiritual path.

Most people believe that there is some type of large goal or purpose for their lives, yet they often don't know what it is or how to follow it. They go through life trying to discover what that purpose is. Some people feel that their purpose is to live a simple yet righteous life and just get by. While others make finding the magic answer a crusade and spend their whole lives reading books and discussing different philosophies searching for the answers. Yet others live average lives and attend church, go to a temple, synagogue, or other place of worship, and occasionally pray to God when they have a question or concern.

People get so caught up looking for the answers that they forget to pay attention to the journey along the way. True, it's important to continue to pray and look for guidance as you continue to discover your purpose or path. That's why it's also necessary to continually ask why and then go to work to solve for how.

As I was saying earlier, we are all born with certain gifts and a divine purpose for our lives. If we continue to ask God for direction and to equip us with the necessary tools to live out that purpose, then He will give us the necessary road maps to follow. These road maps at times may be very subtle or time sensitive. If we are not careful and always listening for directions, we may miss a turn, causing a long detour in our journeys.

Life is made up of many different forces: energy, emotions, wants, needs, and expectations, both good and bad. The questions people ask, and the expectations they have about God's plan, and how they choose to live their lives will help determine the results they receive.

If people believe that life is good and full of great things, this is what they will attract. If they believe that life sucks and the world is out to get them, then that is what they will draw to themselves. It is very important that we monitor our thoughts and feelings because these are the guiding forces that lead us.

God wants people to look to him for guidance, but we have to first choose to do so. Yes, God is within all of us, but because of the influences of the world around everyone, if we aren't careful, it's easy to lose touch with God.

Because God promised people free will, it is that free will which allows us to get into trouble. In the essence of free will, things have the ability to go astray. Even if God wants to intervene - to stay true to His promise - He has to let things run their course. It is our responsibility to live within the framework that God gives us. When we find ourselves outside of that framework, it's important to find ways to get back aligned. That's why prayer is so important. Like it was written in James 1:16, 'But when you ask, you must believe and not doubt, because the one who doubts is like a wave of the sea; blown and tossed by the wind,'" Pistis replied.

"That's a great verse. Years back, Jennifer was having A Crisis of Faith one morning during a heated discussion we were having.

'If what you say about God is true, I wish He would give me a sign. Maybe then I could believe what you're saying,' She yelled as she walked out the door.

She then got in her car, slammed the door, and left. Later that morning, she called me and said that she almost died. 'You almost died, how?'" I asked.

'After I got to work, I had to go to Redmond and pick something up. On my way back to the office, I was getting onto 405 off of 520 and a SUV hit the right side of my car while going 60 miles per hour and caused my car to do a complete 360 sliding across three lanes of traffic and stopping right next to a concrete barrier with just the side of the car touching it.'

'Are you alright?' I asked.

'Yeah, I'm still a little shaken but I'm alright, and the car is alright too."

'Did the car that hit you stop?'

'No, he flew past me, clipped the back side of my car, and kept going. I'm not even sure he knew he hit me.'

Knowing how busy 405 is that time of day and trying to picture Jennifer doing a 360 without hitting anyone or anyone hitting her seemed impossible. 'And you didn't hit any other cars?' I asked.

'No. I don't how but when I started to spin there weren't any cars around me.'

'How about when you hit the concrete barrier, did you bang up the car?' I asked.

'Nope, it was as if there was an invisible hand protecting me from the barrier,' She replied.

'Wow Jennifer! As you know, because of the limousine company, I drive all the time and I see things like that happen quite a bit. First of all, that time of day you should have hit or been hit by someone else. Second of all, when a car does a 360 or spins all the way around on dry pavement going 60 miles per hour it will usually flip over. And when a car going 60 miles per hour manages to slide across three lanes of traffic, even doing a 360 then hits the concrete barrier, the car is almost always totaled. Yet none of those things happened to you. You asked for a sign that God has you in the palm of his hand. I think you got your sign. Please, please don't ask for any more signs, because that was a very radical sign. A burning bush would have been more subtle.'

'Yeah, I guess you have a point,' she said with a slight giggle.

'So was Jennifer's faith strengthened that day?' Pistis asked.

'Yeah, but it's still been a daily struggle.'

"And that's how it is with most people. Walking in faith has to be a daily way of life. Sam, you have given great examples of how you have tried to stay faithful and of times when it was difficult to do. Ways you were rewarded when you stayed true to your own faith yet even then your faith would often be challenged from day to day."

Just then the flight attendant came by with a basket full of snacks. "Yum, more snacks," Pistis said, with a big smile on his face.

With my voice I cry out to the Lord; with my voice I make supplications to the Lord. I pour out my complaints before Him; I tell my troubles before Him. When my spirit is faint, you know my way. – Psalm 142,1-3

CHAPTER 4

A Discussion About Faith

The flight attendant handed us the basket of snacks, asked how we were doing and if we wanted anything to drink. I grabbed a cookie and a bag if sea salt chocolates. Pistis chose a cookie and a bag of potato chips.

"Sam, try to imagine a place where the impossible was possible; where when you closed your eyes and dared to dream, those dreams became your new reality. Imagine a place where you had the power to choose; a place where your destiny was there for the taking. If you were in such a place, would you make different choices as you went through your day?" Pistis asked.

"I don't know, I guess if such a place existed, I would make choices free from worry. I would already know that I was going to get my desired outcome," I answered.

"You see Sam, that's the difference between people and most of nature. In nature, animals move throughout their day not worrying about what's to come. They are instinctual, or habit based. They don't think about whether or not they should do something, or if it will turn out the way they want; they just do it. It's already part of their DNA. However, like I was saying earlier about free will, people are blessed with free will - although some would argue that it's also a curse. Because people have the ability to choose to do something, it takes more effort. That is where faith comes in. Faith is a funny thing; for kids it comes naturally, yet for many adults it is a hard concept to comprehend.

To follow in faith takes a certain amount of trust. One has to yield the feeling of control and trust that all will work out. For many people that is very hard to do. In life, we create certain boundaries that govern the level of control one has. As a society, we put in place laws that create certain boundaries that we learn to live by.

Can you imagine driving a car without traffic rules? We can trust that if we drive down the street in the US, we probably wouldn't feel very safe. We get up and go to work trusting that at the end of the pay period, we will get paid for the work we performed. If the company paid when and if it felt like it, you probably wouldn't show up for work.

Then there are moral guidelines. We can feel confident in most environments that if we leave our houses and walk out into the neighborhood, someone won't walk up to us and try to kill us. As a society, we can put in place many rules or laws. However, in the end, we still need to have faith that people will follow these laws, and everything will work.

Earlier, Sam, you mentioned the law of attraction. About how if we visualize a certain outcome, we can attract it into our lives. Whether you call it faith, visualization or something else, in the end if you truly believe it's possible, you can attract it into your life. That doesn't mean you can just sit there, picture it, and it will come. You still have to take the necessary steps to bring it about.

The degree of your faith, and the proactive actions that you take, will determine how quickly it will become realty. The true challenge comes from faith's ugly brother, fear. Both can be very strong emotions. Both can be very powerful and move you towards a great life, or push greatness away from you just as fast. And if not properly managed, both can cause you to live a life full of regret," Pistis explained, as he opened the bag of potato chips the flight attendant had just given him.

"I know what you mean. I often tell our kids that in life we can't always control our results. However, we can control our activities. When we do the right activities, (granted it may take time, patience, and the help of other people), in time we will receive our desired results.

I remember some years back when Sabrina was in the Milwaukee Youth Symphony Orchestra, or MYSO. She played the flute in a group called Chamber Flutes, which was made up of different flautists. She set a goal of becoming a member of a group called the Philharmonic Orchestra, which is very hard to get into.

Sabrina had to try out, and then wait for about a month before she knew if she got in. The day the results arrived, Sabrina was having lunch with a friend of hers, who was already in the Philharmonic Orchestra. They were at a restaurant a few blocks from our house.

Two letters came in the mail from MYSO and knowing how bad Sabrina had wanted to know the results, I decided to bring them to her. Sabrina opened the first letter and saw that she had made it back into Chamber Flutes. She then opened the second letter and sat there with tears running down her cheeks.

'Why, Dad, why? I wanted to get into the Philharmonic Orchestra so bad.'

'I know, Sabrina.'

'I got wait-listed. Why? I practiced so much!'

'I don't know, Sabrina. What I do know is that in life we get three answers: Yes, no, or not now. It's not yes, because you didn't get in yet. It's not no, because you're wait-listed. So that just means that it's *not now*. Maybe you will have to wait until next year or, maybe later this year. Remember, you can't always control the results, but you can control your actions.'

'Do me a favor, Sabrina,' I said, hugging her, 'You have Chamber Flutes from 4:30 to 6:00 on Mondays, and the Philharmonic Orchestra practices from 6:30 to 9:00 on Mondays, Right?'

'Yes, Dad, that's right.'

'Since you're going to be there anyway, why don't you go to the Philharmonic Orchestra, help set up, talk with your friends, and envision how you would feel and what you would be doing if you were in the orchestra, okay?'

'Okay, Dad.'

The first week of practice arrived, and Sabrina helped set up. Her friends came in and she talked and joked around with them. She stood where she would stand if she had gotten into the orchestra. She visualized how she would feel if she were part of the orchestra.

Then it was time for the orchestra to start, so we had to leave. Sabrina walked out, looking down at the ground with a sad look on her face. The second week came, and we repeated the process, and again when it was time for the orchestra to start, Sabrina left with a sad look on her face. The third week came, and we repeated the process, and again it was time for the orchestra to start and Sabrina left with a sad look on her face.

I was starting to second-guess myself. I couldn't help thinking that I might unintentionally be setting Sabrina up for continued disappointment. I hated to see her leave looking so down in the dumps. I asked Sabrina if she liked to help set up and hang out with her friends.

She answered, 'Yes, I would rather be in the room helping to set up than not at all. I just really wish I could stay and play with the orchestra.'

I told her to be patient and her turn would come. The following week, Sabrina was at a swim meet. While I was waiting for her, I got a call from the senior conductor for the Philharmonic Orchestra, who said, 'Mike, I opened up another seat for Sabrina, and I would really like her to play with us.' Then he asked if she would still like to be part of the orchestra.

I said, 'Yes, she has been praying every day for this opportunity. I will let her know and we will see you on Monday.'

'Great! I look forward to seeing Sabrina next week,' he said.

Not only did she finish out the year in the Philharmonic Orchestra, she won a contest and was able to compose a piece for the Chamber Flutes.

In 2012, she got into the highest-level at the Milwaukee Youth Symphony Orchestra, called Senior Symphony. The summer of her senior year of high school, they toured Vienna and Prague and represented the United States in an international music contest, where they placed second in the world.

I taught our kids that once visualized, goals are very powerful motivators. The only challenge both adults and children run into when they have a really large goal, is that it can become overwhelming. It's hard to determine what to do first. So, I would tell them the first step to avoid being overwhelmed is to see the goal as if it has already been completed. The next step is to back-engineer the steps to the beginning.

As an example, my younger daughter, Monica, has wanted a puppy since she was around ten. About once a month, she would ask Jennifer and me if we could get a puppy. Jennifer always answered, 'No, Monica, we already have three fish. A puppy is too much work.'

When Monica was thirteen, she found a really cute puppy and brought a picture to show us. 'Mom, Dad, look at this puppy. It's so cute, and it only costs $750. Can I get it? Please, please can I get it? I'll pay for it.'

Now, when your 14-year-old daughter says 'only $750' when talking about a dog (puppy or not), that should be the first reason to worry.

Jennifer looked at Monica, and said, '$750, huh? And you will pay for it?'

'Yes, only $750. I'll pay for it and we can pick it up in four weeks.'

'Okay, tell you what,' Jennifer replied, 'You have three weeks to come up with the money, and you can't take any money out of your bank account. You have to raise the money from scratch.'

'Really, then I can have my puppy?'

'That's correct,' Jennifer said.

'Okay, Mom, let me fill this out and then please sign it.' Monica grabbed a pen and wrote out the following.

I, Jennifer Raber, will let Monica Raber buy her puppy if she can raise the money within three weeks. Jennifer signed the sheet and gave it back to Monica. I think that Jennifer secretly hoped Monica would say, 'Raise $750 in three weeks from scratch? That's impossible. Okay, then, I guess I can't have the puppy.'

Jennifer must have forgotten that since our children were small, we have instilled in them the belief that if there is something they want, it's a sound purchase, and they have the ability to raise the money to buy it; if they set a goal to get the thing that they want, we would support their decision and help them figure out a way to raise the money.

Monica started to back-engineer her goal: $750 in three weeks. That would be $250 a week or $35.71 a day. Now she just needed a way to earn the money.

Sabrina and I would teach seminars to kids and their parents on how to develop sound money management habits. We would use a special bank which was divided into three sections for spending, sharing, and saving.

Monica figured if she could sell one bank for a profit of $5, she would have to sell a total of 150 banks, or 50 banks a week, or 7.14 banks a day.

Later that day, Monica called the breeder and negotiated him down to six hundred and fifty dollars. She then asked me if she could go to different networking meetings with me so she could sell the banks. I said, 'Yes', and she was able to raise the money in just short of three weeks.

Monica is now the proud owner of a black Cockapoo puppy named Lucy. I have to admit that I'm really glad Monica had her dream of getting a puppy, and that she went for it and brought Lucy into our family. Lucy is the cutest puppy and often sleeps on the floor next to me," I said smiling.

"Wow, those sure are great examples of staying faithful to one's dream," Pistis said, chuckling.

"Yeah, I guess goal setting and staying true to one's faith has been a big part of our family's culture. That's probably why the verse, 'Trust in the Lord with all your heart, and lean on your own understanding: in all your ways submit to Him, and He will make your paths straight' Has always been one of my favorite verses," I said.

"Oh yes, Proverbs 3:5-6; that's a good one."

Be on your guard, stand firm in the faith, be courageous: Be strong.' - 1 Corinthians 16:13. And, 'Now faith is confidence in what we hope for and assurance about what we do not see.' Hebrews 11:1, are two more great verses," Pistis said with a large smile.

"It's wise to be skeptical and it's natural to ask why. But in the end, as people continue to find their way, it's important to stay faithful and have patience that God's divine glory will shine through them. Sam, when was a time in your life when you had to stay true to your own faith, and step outside of what felt safe on a true leap of faith?" Pistis asked as he took a bite out of another potato chip.

Love is patient, love is kind. It does not envy, it does not boast, it is not proud. It does not dishonor others, it is not self-seeking, it is not easily angered, it keeps no record of wrongs.
- 1 Corinthians 13:4-5

CHAPTER 5

A Journey Across the World

"I guess probably the best example of a time when I had to step outside of my comfort zone, away from all that felt safe and take a huge leap of faith, would be when I went to Taiwan," I replied.

"It all started shortly after I finished tenth grade. I moved back to Milwaukee after my dad asked me to move back in with my mom. I ended up going to a small independent high school on the south side of Milwaukee and finished tenth grade there. The school didn't do very much for my basic education, but I became friends with the school counselor. Over the course of the year, he had me read approximately twenty books on psychology. I really liked the subject and would often self-diagnose myself and those around me.

At the start of the next school year, I wanted to transfer back to the Milwaukee Public School System. However, the school district wouldn't recognize the classes I had taken over the last year because I had gone to a small, independent school. That meant I would have to redo tenth grade.

I couldn't believe it; here I was once again being told that I would have to redo a school year. Enough was enough, so I started to explore my options. At the time, if a person took the GED (or General Equivalency Diploma) exam, and scored over 290, he or she could get into any state college. I knew I would need to go to college at some point.

Plus, ever since I gave my testimony at the Brown Deer Baptist fall church camp, I couldn't stop thinking about the feeling I had as I stood there and watched person after person walk up in front of the camp and commit their lives to Christ. I knew there was something much greater that God had planned for my life. So, I would likely have to go to college. I figured if I could score over 290 on the GED, I could get into a local community college. I took the GED test and scored above that."

"Wow sounds like giving your testimony and seeing God's radiance, or as you put it, 'Gods divine glory,' shine through you helped to reveal Gods true grace that lives inside of you," Pistis said laughing.

"Yeah, I guess that's very true. Well, anyway back to how I ended up in Taiwan. Henry Chang, a friend of the family, owned a Chinese restaurant on the east side of Milwaukee, where I worked part-time after school as a prep cook and dishwasher. Since I no longer needed a high school diploma to get into college, I dropped out of high school and went to work at the restaurant full time.

I then took some evening classes at the local community college and continued to work on a plan for the dream business that came to me in seventh grade. The more I worked for the restaurant, the more I knew Henry would be able to help make my dream a reality. Because of all the time I spent with my stepfather John, and his being a chef in some of the finest restaurants and hotels in Milwaukee, I came to really like the restaurant business.

I wanted to learn how to cook Chinese food and later open a Chinese restaurant as part of my dream enterprise. I would often ask Henry to teach me how to cook. He would laugh and say, 'You're not Chinese, so how can you open a Chinese restaurant?'

One day, Ti-man the head cook, and I went fishing after work and I was sharing my frustrations with him. I told him, 'I don't get it. I'm a hard worker, I grew up in the restaurant business and I know that I would make a great business owner. What does my not being Chinese have to do with anything?' I asked with a loud sigh.

Smiling, Ti-man started to explain that it wasn't me. He could tell that Henry really liked and respected me. But there are some strong traditions that Chinese live by. For a Chinese to teach a non-Chinese how to cook would be in a way a violation of a silent code.'

'You mean like when the famous actor Bruce Lee said he wanted to teach Chinese Kung Fu to non-Chinese?' I asked.

'Correct, there are those who believe such things should only be taught to or done by other Chinese.'

'I see, but I only want to learn in honor of what the Chinese have accomplished and because I love Chinese food and want to share it with others,' I replied.

'I know, but traditions can be very hard to let go of, especially when the tradition is connected to some kind of silent code,' Ti-man replied.

A couple of weeks later, Ti-man decided to teach me how to cook Chinese food. However, he also knew he couldn't openly show me how, so he would do things like knock over a bag of flour, and then tell me to clean it up. As I cleaned up the flour, he would recite the recipe out loud as he made the dish. Then he told me to go home and practice. One could say that I learned the entire menu on my hands and knees while cleaning something up. The kitchen staff and I worked during the day then after closing the restaurant around 10PM, Henry and I would sit around discussing different business ideas.

A truly wonderful teacher, Ti-man also told me that if I really wanted to open a Chinese restaurant; because I wasn't Chinese, I would need to develop the inner strength to be able to overcome any obstacle that came my way. So, he had me do different Chinese Kung Fu exercises. Every morning, he had me crush up ten large bus pans full of cooked rice that had been in the walk-in freezer overnight, using my bare hands to squeeze the blocks of rice until they crumbled.

One day, after complaining that my hands really hurt, Ti-man walked over to me, grabbed a handful of rice, and squeezed it as it fell back into the bus pan. He then turned, moved his hand in front of him in what looked like a tiger's claw, and struck a box full of broccoli on the counter in front of us. Without even moving the box, he then pulled his hand back, leaving five perfect holes in the box where his fingers had penetrated it! Looking at me with a smile on his face, he said, 'No pain, no gain. It is through hard work and learning to embrace the pain that true mastery resides,' and walked away.

In winter, during my lunch breaks, he also had me go outside into the alley behind the restaurant without a shirt in 30-degree weather. There, I practiced a tiger form until my *chi*, or vital energy, kept my body warm. Both Henry Chang and Ti-man were great mentors.

"One of the things about working at Henry Chang's was that I had a strong passion for Chinese culture and martial arts, for as long as I can remember. But somehow, when Karen and I broke up, I went into a mental hibernation mode. After dropping out of high school, only three things mattered to me, winning Karen back, becoming a master of Chinese Kung Fu, and at some point, opening a Chinese restaurant which meant I needed to learn how to cook Chinese food."

"Outside of winning Karen back, those are some odd goals for a kid coming from your background," Pistis said.

"I know. That's what's so odd about it all. None of it really made any sense. There were a number of things that I should have been doing, given my family and upbringing. Yet none of it seemed to really matter. It was as if I was being directed by some outside force," I said

"Over the years my love for Chinese culture and Chinese Kung Fu became stronger and stronger. At times, the only time I felt completely at peace was when I was practicing Kung Fu. In fact, between studying with Ti-Man, working at Henry Chang's, and practicing Kung Fu, I knew there was still something out there beyond my reach. I often dreamed about being in the Shaolin Temple practicing with the masters, yet I couldn't stop thinking about Karen.

I often found myself praying for guidance. My friends would tell me that I needed to forget about Karen and start dating other girls. On the surface it made perfect sense. So, I would ask a girl I had just met out on a date, but when I was with her, I couldn't stop thinking about Karen. So, I'd politely end the date and go back to practicing Chinese Kung Fu.

Four months after I turned 18, I ran into Matt, my childhood best friend from across the alley. He was going to college at UW-Stevens Point at the time. We were talking and he invited me to come visit him there.

I decided to take him up on his offer, borrowed a friend's car and drove up to see him.

It turned out Karen was also going to Stevens Point. As luck would have it, while I was there visiting Matt, I bumped into her outside of her class. It was the craziest thing! Even though I hadn't seen Karen since 10th grade, it was like I had just seen her yesterday. She asked what I was doing there, and I told her I was visiting a friend and that I was thinking of going to school there too.

Well anyway, we said our goodbyes and Karen said that I should really think about going there, that Stevens Point was a great school and that it would be great to have an old friend there. She then gave me her phone number, told me to call her if I ended up going there, and walked into class. Matt and I hung out for the rest of the weekend and I went back to Milwaukee."

"So, then what? Something tells me that's not the end of the story," Pistis asked.

"You're right. I couldn't stop thinking about her. I called my sister and explained my dilemma, and she simply said, 'Then why don't you go there? You said that you wanted to go to college at some point. So why not go there?'

'You're right,' I said, and I enrolled the next week.

The beginning of the spring semester was about to begin. My Mom drove me to Stevens Point and helped me check into my dorm. We said our goodbyes and the next week I started school.

A week after I moved into the dorm, I called Karen and we went out for dinner. It was magical. I told her about my vision for the business, and she said that she couldn't believe how innovative it was. We talked every day. She shared many stories about what she had been up to the past couple of years. I told her about Ti-Man and the multiple lessons he had shared with me.

About a month into the semester, I invited her to my dorm where I cooked her a five course Chinese dinner. It was like time had stopped. Everything I had dreamed of, since my dad called Karen's mom that one night, was quickly becoming reality. I learned how to cook Chinese food, I had become pretty good at Chinese Kung Fu and I was once again winning Karen's heart. Life was great!

Then one afternoon, a few months later over a cup of coffee, the unbelievable happened. Karen set her coffee cup down, leaned forward in her chair, took my hand, and said she had really enjoyed the last couple of months we spent together but that she wanted to see other people and that she didn't think she could do that and see me at the same time. Her feelings for me were too strong. So, she didn't think we should see each other for a while.

The bottom just fell out of my world. Two weeks had gone by with no phone calls, no passing her in the hallway, nothing. It was as if she had fallen off the face of the earth - well my earth anyway. Then I was invited to a church event with some friends in my dorm and there she was. I felt this warm glow come over me as I walked up to her and said 'Hi.'

'Hi,' she replied, as she turned and walked away.

I stood there stunned. 'What just happened?' I kept thinking to myself. I must have looked like a confused puppy, because just then Karen's mom walked over to me from across the room and gave me a hug. She then looked me in the eyes and said, 'I don't know what to say, except that this isn't easy for her either. Right now she needs her space and as hard as it is to accept, for right now you need to be the man I know you are and give her that space.'

As tears started to roll down my cheeks, I looked at her and said, 'But she just came back into my life?'

'I know, I really like you Mike, I always have. But in the end, it has to be something that Karen wants too. And right now, that's not the case.'

'I don't understand why we can't still be friends. I just want her in my life, for now that would be enough.'

'Sam, unfortunately, the only way Karen can deal with her feelings is by not seeing you. Otherwise, it hurts her too much.'

Looking up at Karen's mom, I replied, 'It still doesn't make any sense to me, but I pray that someday it will. Thank you for your continual guidance. You have always been like a mom to me, and for that I will be forever grateful.' I then said my goodbyes to my friends there and walked back to my dorm.

It was like time once again came to a standstill. I was so angry. It wasn't fair; life wasn't fair. Every time my life seemed to be going well and I was truly happy, something would happen causing it to be turned upside down. I tried to be faithful; to do what I thought was right, yet it never seemed to be enough. I felt like I was continually being punished for something I didn't even understand," I said to Pistis with a long sigh.

"Sam, sometimes what feels like a punishment is actually the preparation for something coming that will be even better. It's like if you want to run a marathon but you haven't even run a mile, you will have to train for a while first. As first, running will be both mentally and physically painful, but without pushing through it, you won't survive the marathon.

Life is that same way, we might think we are poised for something great and enjoying each day as it comes, yet there is something far better to receive, or more important for us to accomplish. Life has a way of conditioning us to be able to handle what is to come. And yes, it is often painful. And yes, it can often feel like we are being punished for something we don't understand. And yes, it isn't always fair, but it's our becoming who we need to be for which we can become truly great," Pistis replied.

"I guess that makes sense, but all I knew was I needed answers and I needed them yesterday. Sitting at my desk, with tears streaming down my face, I thought back to when John told me that sometimes in order to truly understand ourselves, we must first learn to become one with nature.

There was an old ranger station in a nature reserve about six blocks from my dorm that was four stories tall. You could walk up the first three stories, but the last story was chained off so people couldn't climb to the top. It was perfect. What better way to become one with nature then to sit there and meditate under the stars? There it sat in the middle of a nature reserve free from all human interaction. Four stories up in the air wide open under the stars, and no one would bother me because they couldn't see me.

It was the perfect place, except for the small detail that I would have to somehow make it past the chains in order to get to the fourth story. Oh, and it was averaging between 20 and 30 degrees outside. And if it should snow, which was likely, there wasn't any roof as it was the top story, so it would snow on me while I was meditating."

"Sounds like a recipe for disaster. So why do I have a feeling that you found a way to get up there anyway?" Pistis said, laughing.

"Yep, so I gathered up all my stuff, waited until about 11:30pm so I could be sure that no one was around. I then went to the reserve, climbed the first three stories and examined the chains. I came to the conclusion that I could use a rope I brought with me to catapult my gear over the ledge and up to the top level. I then slowly moved the chain back and forth until I could get just enough room to slowly slide my body through the opening. Voila! There I was, all alone, nothing but me and the stars. It was magical. Sure, it was very cold, but the night sky was crystal clear exposing every star's truest beauty."

"Wow! That sounds very ingenious, yet crazy. Then again so have most of the stories you have been sharing with me. So, you obviously didn't freeze to death. Did you learn to become one with nature? And how long did you stay there for?" Pistis asked

"Nope, I didn't freeze to death. My stepfather taught me how to dress to keep out the cold, and Ti-Man taught me how to breathe in order to keep in my vital heat. And over time, yes in a way, I guess I did become closer to nature. I went back to the ranger station each night until I started to feel at peace with once again losing Karen. Only this time, I had come to believe that we truly weren't meant to be together. That somehow, I was meant to answer to a different calling."

"Sounds like a great testament of the power of the Holy Spirit working in your life. It reminds me of this verse: John 3:8 , 'The wind blows wherever it pleases. You hear its sound, but you cannot tell where it comes from or where it's going. So to it is with everyone born of the Spirit'," Pistis replied.

"Yep, that became the start of a wild couple of months."

"What do you mean?" Pistis asked.

"While I was at the ranger station meditating, or what might better be referred to as having a long conversation with God through prayer, I had this overwhelming feeling come over me that I needed to travel to Asia in search of my mission. Not understanding why, I thought about my dream of joining the Shaolin Temple. Yet somehow that didn't feel right. I didn't know how, when, or why, just that it felt very real. There were only two more days left of the semester. The whole next day I couldn't stop thinking about the feeling I had the night before, and how it didn't really make any sense.

I decided to share the vision with Steve, one of my friends from the church I would go to sometimes. I guess I kind of hoped he would tell me I was crazy and to let it go."

"And, what did he say?"

"That's the crazy thing, he sat there quiet at first. Then he quoted a verse to me, 'Hear now my words: if there is a prophet among you. I, the Lord, shall make Myself known to him a vision I shall speak with him in a dream'."

"Ah, Numbers 12:6," Pistis said smiling.

"You know that one?" I asked, surprised.

"Ah yes, that's a classic. So, what did Steve say next?"

"Steve followed by asking. 'So, are you thinking about making such a trip?'

'I don't know, but knowing that it's the last day of school, I don't think that I will be returning after the break.'

'Really you think you might be going that soon?' Steve asked, with a surprised look on his face.

'Well that's the problem; a month ago I was in seventh heaven. I had won back Karen's heart. I was once again doing well in school. Now Karen won't even look at me, and when I'm praying for guidance I get a vision that I'm supposed to move to the other side of the world. None of this makes any sense anymore. That's why I was hoping it might make sense to you, Steve, given how well you understand the Bible.'

'Sam, do you feel like the Holy Spirit is currently working in you? Or do you feel like the idea, this new journey is totally crazy?' Steve asked.

'I don't know what I feel, yet somehow it feels so right, that's the problem.'

'Do you really believe that this, your vision, is something you have to do, and if so, are you are prepared to do it?'

'Yes, I know that I have to stay true to my path no matter how strange it might seem. Do I feel ready? Honestly, I just feel confused; really, really confused. I would give anything to just close my eyes and when I open them, I would be back in my dorm room sitting across from Karen eating the dinner I just made for her.'

I couldn't hold it back any longer; I just started to shake then broke down and sobbed. Steve put his hand on my shoulder and said this prayer, 'May the God of hope fill you with joy and peace as you trust in Him, so that you may overflow with hope by the power of the Holy Spirit'."

"Ah yes, Romans 15:13, another classic," Pistis said chuckling.

Surprised that he knew that one too, I continued with my story. "So, as I started to regain my composure, Steve told me to wait there, that he would be right back. He then got up and left the room. About 45 minutes later, he returned and told me to follow him.

'Ok, but where are we going?'

'You'll see, just come with me,' Steve said, as we got into his car.

A few minutes later, we pulled into the church parking lot, got out of his car, and entered the church. I stood there in complete disbelief. Almost everyone who was in a Bible study Steve and I were part of was standing inside of the church waiting for us. What was this, some sort of spiritual intervention? Somehow, in less than ninety minutes, he was able to get everyone there including the Pastor and Karen's mom, which in its own right was just short of a miracle. Not to mention the fact that it was now 2:00 o'clock in the morning.

The Pastor walked over to me and told me that Steve had called him and shared with him what he and I had been talking about. He then told Steve that if I truly believed that it was a big enough calling from God to send me unknowingly across the world in search of the answer, then I needed to bring with me the armor of God.

'The armor of God, what is that and how do I get it?' I asked Pastor.

'Follow me Sam,' The pastor said as we walked over to this large tank full of water.

'It's the ultimate blessing, or favor of the Holy Spirit. And how you get it is first by asking for it through prayer, and then sealing it by being baptized.' The pastor said.

'Yeah, but I have already been baptized,' I replied

'I know, and that was to show your love for the Lord and to accept Him into your life. This time it is to show your total faith and willingness to follow in His calling no matter how hard that may be. And from that you will carry with you his favor whenever the time for your calling arises. However, once requested, it's very important that you pay close attention to what ever signs may arise. Sam do you accept this calling and act of faithfulness?'

'Yes, I accept, Pastor.'

'Ok then Sam, step down into this tank, close your eyes while asking God for his favor as I lean you back into the water.'

'Ok' And I started to pray for God's favor, protection. And continued guidance as I became completely submerged under the water.

"Wow sounds like you were in the arms of some very godly people. Not very many people can say they were baptized twice!" Pistis said, with a big smile on his face.

"That is very true! So I dried myself off and stood there with this huge sense of peace flowing through me, as person after person came up to me wished me luck and said, 'God be with you.'

The semester came to an end, I went back to Milwaukee and started working at Henry Chang's again as I waited for my next move. Only this time things seemed different. Shortly after my nineteenth birthday, and probably the five-hundredth time asking Henry to help me open a Chinese restaurant and his responding with, 'But you're not Chinese,' I finally angrily requested that he teach me how to become Chinese. It couldn't be that difficult, for there were already two billion Chinese people on the planet.

Annoyed, he finally said, 'Okay, this is the deal. You have two weeks to get ready. If you move to Taiwan and stay there for five years, when you return, I will help you open a restaurant. However, you can only buy a one-way ticket and take one hundred dollars with you. You have to be able to survive there for at least five years.'

'Really ... if I do that,' I stuttered, 'in five years, you will help me open a Chinese restaurant?'

'Yes,' he said.

'Ok, then,' I said, 'I will see you in five years. By the way, I am giving you my two-week notice.' I think he thought I would respond to his suggestion with words to the extent of,

'Are you crazy? I don't know anyone in Taiwan, and I can't speak Chinese. I will starve to death.' At least that is what everyone else said when I told them what I was going to do. All I knew was, the vision I had that night at the ranger station had somehow prepared me for the journey I was about to begin. And if Henry helped me open a restaurant, it would be the first leg of my dream. As long as I continued to believe that I was following God's plan. I wasn't going to let anything stand in the way.

I was nineteen. Henry knew that my mom didn't have very much money, so I wouldn't ask her for money to get back. I would have no way home. So, giving up wasn't an option, which meant if I wanted to survive, I would have to learn to think like a Chinese very quickly. He also knew that I would do anything it took as long as it was legal and ethical until I reached my goal. Taiwan would be an amazing place for continuing to learn and work on my dream.

The next day, after shock of what I had just agreed to started to wear off, I was shooting pool in a bar down the street from Henry Chang with some friends. I decided to tell my friends about my deciding to go Taiwan and the journey I was about to embark on. Amazingly, after a couple of pitchers of beer and a few games of pool, I somehow had convinced two of my friends, John and Eli, to come with me. We decided that John and I would fly there together, and Eli would meet us there later, as he still needed to get a passport.

Soon after landing In Taiwan, I discovered that with the right attitude, one can do almost anything. It was the beginning of a series of life changing challenges that I would be faced with having to somehow overcome.

My friend John and I were living in an International Youth Hostel near the largest university in Taipei. The first eight floors were set up similar to college dorm rooms, and were rented by the month. The ninth floor had rooms with ten bunk beds in them that were rented by the day.

We rented a two-person room on the fifth floor. I made a deal with the owner of a Chinese restaurant that was across the street from the International Youth Hostel to work for free in exchange for free food, and the cooks would teach me how to cook. I was starting to settle in and getting used to living in Taiwan. Then as my savings quickly started to run out, we weren't able to pay our rent and had to move. There I was, living the dream and homeless. I wanted to keep working at the restaurant, but the owner couldn't afford to pay me, and I didn't really want to sleep outside.

People who stayed on the ninth floor, of the International Youth Hostel would come and go, it was hard to tell who was paying month to month or by the day. There was a guard in the lobby who would keep a window open and always took a nap at 2:00am each day.

John and I would find things to do to keep ourselves busy, then at 2:00am climb in through the window, go up to the ninth floor, find two beds and go to sleep. We were able to repeat that for a couple of months, and then John got an opportunity to move in with his Kung Fu teacher. I had a small teaching job, teaching business English to a company that printed cardboard boxes. One day after class was over, I shared with the owners about how I needed to find another place to live. They told me that if I wanted, they had a small storeroom in the back of the factory that I could stay in until I was able to find a better place."

"You stayed in a small storeroom? Where did you sleep?" Pistis asked.

"Well, it wasn't the Ritz Carlton that's for sure, but they had a small storage chest that was like a five-foot by ten-foot stage that they stored things in. I was able to make the stage part into a make-shift bed. I put a thick blanket down and slept on that. Except for the occasional man-eating cock roach crawling across my bed, it was always warm, dry, and certainly better than a park bench," I answered.

"How long did you stay there for?"

"For about six months. The only challenge with staying there was they locked the door every day at 10:00pm, slid a large metal door down over the entrance, and everyone would go home. So, if I got back later than that I would get locked out. One night I walked Jennifer home from school, said my goodbyes, and got on my bus only to have the bus break down. I didn't make it back until 10:45pm. The door was locked, and everyone had already gone home."

"What did you do?"

"Well, I stood there in shock for a few minutes, then I figured I would buy a few bottles of beer, go behind the factory, where they had a small patio and figure out what to do next. I sat down on a bench and started drinking my beer. After finishing my second beer, I watched a cat that lived in the factory walk past me, jump up on to a ledge, follow that ledge to another one, jump onto a second story ledge, and go in through a window that was open about halfway.

I finished my third and last beer and thought to myself, 'If the cat can do that, then why can't I?' I stood up, scaled the side of the building, went in through the window, jumped down and there I was next to my room.

It seemed like a good idea at that moment, but my students heard about my adventure from a neighbor and suggested that I find another place to stay. The next week, I was able to sublet a room from a classmate of mine.

Another major challenge came the first time I had to go to Hong Kong. I was running out of money and wasn't able to continue to pay for school, which meant that I would lose my student visa.

After a week or two of having an expired visa, I figured I had better go to the foreign affairs office and find out what my options were. The immigration officer told me that I needed to leave the country and go to Hong Kong to renew my visa. However, I wasn't able to leave Taiwan with an expired visa, at least not on a commercial airline.

Taiwan is an island, and I certainly didn't really want to swim from Taiwan to Hong Kong. After what felt like hours, the immigration officer noticed that I was from Wisconsin. He suddenly perked up and said that he and his family had visited Wisconsin the previous summer.

One of the highlights of the trip was going to a cheese factory there. The officer told me that he really liked string cheese, and at that time, it wasn't possible to buy string cheese anywhere in Taiwan. Jokingly, I said, 'Hey, if I come back in a week with a case of string cheese, would you help me reevaluate my dilemma?'

The immigration officer smiled and told me to go home and come back in a week. (In Taiwan, those words are code for 'Yeah, that's a great idea') I left the office, went home, called my mother and told her that I needed a case of string cheese or would likely go to jail. After a series of questions, my mom sent me the case of string cheese and I went back to the foreign affairs office.

The immigration officer watched me walk in and told me to put the case of string cheese down on the counter. I was also to give him my passport. The immigration officer came back after a few minutes, told me that he must have looked at the visa wrong during the last visit, and that my visa actually expired the following day. This meant that I could catch the first flight out of Taiwan and go to Hong Kong.

I couldn't believe it; my visa was no longer expired. All I had to do was go to Hong Kong, then return and my visa would be good for another two months. As long as I could get into a Chinese school within the two months, I could renew my visa without having to leave the country.

I went back to where I was staying, scraped together all my money, and had just enough to buy a plane ticket. Some students of mine, who I was living with at the time, loaned me 1,000 Taiwan dollars or roughly 25 US dollars for spending money while I was in Hong Kong.

The next day, I was on my way to Hong Kong. Everything was going along just as planned, until I realized that the average cost per night for a hotel room was 100 US dollars, and I had to stay in Hong Kong for three nights. I went to six different hotels trying to find a room, and the cheapest one was 75 dollars.

I sat down a bench in front of one of the hotels. Worry started to set in. What would I do? I didn't really want to sleep on a park bench. Living the hobo life was a challenge in America, let alone in a foreign country. I decided to get something to eat and pray for direction. I saw a sign down the street that said beef noodle soup, so I stood up and started walking towards it. As I approached the noodle stand, I looked down an alley next to the stand and there was a bright orange sign with yellow neon letters that read, 'Ping's Hostel'

Something about that moment seemed so natural, so I turned and walked down the alley to a red door just below the sign and rang the bell. The door opened and standing in the doorway was a middle-aged lady. Seeing that I was most likely from The United States, she said, 'Sorry, I only speak little English.'

Forgetting for a moment that I was in Hong Kong, I asked her in Mandarin.

'Good evening ma'am, do you have any rooms available?'

'Yes, we have space available,' the lady answered in Mandarin with a large smile. She then asked me if I could speak Mandarin.

'Yes, I can speak some Mandarin,' I replied.

'Good evening, my name is Mrs. Ping. Are you American?' She asked.

'Yes, my name is Sam. I'm glad to meet you. How much does it cost to stay here?' I asked with a worried look on my face.

'It's only 35 Hong Kong dollars (five US dollars) per night,' She answered.

A huge sense of relief came over me. We stood there in the doorway for probably thirty minutes talking. She told me that she was from China, and she and her husband had moved to Hong Kong five years ago. She said that she couldn't speak Cantonese or English very well, so it was hard for her to find people to talk to. She told me that she would often get very lonely, so she was so happy I came by.

It was so strange; here I was in a foreign country, speaking a language that wasn't mine and that I wasn't very fluent in. Yet, it was the first time I felt at home since I arrived in Taiwan. Maybe it was because I felt stranded, and I too was alone. Somehow talking to Mrs. Ping felt so safe. Someone who was staying at the hostel there came up and asked Mrs. Ping a question in broken English. She answered his question, then realized that we had been standing in the doorway talking and invited me in for tea.

We sat there, drinking tea and talking, for another hour or so. Mrs. Ping said she was tired and asked if I wanted to stay there. 'Yes, that would be great,' I said giving her enough money for one night. I then got up, excused myself and walked into my room.

Even though I had stayed at other hostels before, I wasn't totally sure what to expect. Sometimes, you got your own room, although they were very small. The last one I stayed at had enough room for a single bed and maybe a foot or so on each side of the bed. Then there was a bathroom that everyone shared. And sometimes the hostel would have a large room with many beds in it.

Ping's hostel had a large room with ten bunk beds in it. The biggest challenge with a shared room is you have to continually guard your stuff. I went into the room put my backpack under my bed, lay down and remembered back to when John (my step father) would tell stories of how when you sleep you always have to keep one eye open."

"How do you sleep with one eye open?" Pistis asked.

"That's a good question. John would say that you have to train yourself to let your sub-conscious mind, the part of your brain that's used for healing, fully rest; while your conscious mind is monitoring everything going on around you."

"Assuming you're able to do that, how will that help you?" Pistis asked.

"John would say that when you're in the field, sleep is very important for your survival, yet if you sleep too soundly, you may end up with a knife in your chest or your fire arm taken, leaving you in harm's way," I answered.

"But how would that apply to you?" Pistis asked

"Well that's the strange part. Even though I didn't carry a firearm or wasn't in a war zone for that matter, I did carry my passport, plane ticket back to Taiwan, and any money I had. So, if that got stolen, I would be in a world of hurt. Even though I wasn't in the military and I was never faced with being shot at or many of the horrors of being in the field, every day since I had left the United States, I woke up wondering if I would survive the day. And, often I would reflect on the many stories that John had shared with me.

For that reason, I will always have the utmost respect for those who do join the military and other protective occupations. They put themselves through the toughest training, and often very uncomfortable and dangerous situations so they are able to watch over the freedom of the common person. To protect a freedom that we are all promised, but often never fully appreciate. Such as my friend Joe, a Seattle fire fighter, other fire fighters, police officers, and the many other law enforcement professionals who risk their lives on a daily basis for the protection or those around them.

Anyway, back to the story of Ping's hostel. So, I walked into the room, lay down in the bed that was assigned to me, and fell asleep only to be awakened to the sound of two drunken guys stumbling into the room and falling into their beds. I drifted off to sleep and was once again awakened by the sound of a cat fighting what seemed like a much larger animal in the alley below my window.

Then, after a few minutes I fell back to sleep only to be awakened by a rat sitting in the middle of my room eating something. I lay there watching the rat and fell back to sleep. A short while later I was awakened by a two-inch cock roach crawling across my chest! I flicked it off my chest and got up. Enough was enough; I couldn't take it anymore.

I went outside and walked across the street to a small convenience store, bought a six pack of beer which came to a whopping three US dollars, went back to Ping's hostel and drank the beer in the stairwell. I finished the beer and decided to see if there was anything to eat. To my surprise, there was a McDonald's that was open twenty-four hours a day. I went over to the McDonalds, bought a Filet-O-Fish, and sat down at a table in the back of the restaurant. I put my head down on my backpack, so I knew that it was safe, and quickly drifted off to sleep.

I woke up four hours later shocked at how no bothered me.

The next morning, I explored my options. I had enough money to buy three more meals and stay at Ping's hostel. Or I could buy a six pack of beer and find somewhere to drink it. Then go to the McDonald's next to Ping's hostel, buy a Filet-O-Fish sandwich, find a quiet place to sit down and go to sleep in the back of the restaurant.

I picked the second choice. I really liked Mrs. Ping, but it was clear that I wasn't going to get any sleep there. For the next two days I walked around exploring the sights, went to the small convenience store, bought a six pack of beer, went to a nearby park, drank it, went to McDonalds and fell asleep.

Two days later, I boarded the plane and went back to Taiwan."

"Wow, that's the first time I heard of McDonald's being used as a hotel. Sounds like you learned to become very resilient," Pistis said, laughing.

"Yeah, in many ways, I guess I did. All I know is I returned to Taiwan with a new understanding of the term 'free enterprise', which became one of the many things I came to love during my stay in Taiwan. Over the next several years in Taiwan, I learned valuable lessons about business and life. There were many challenges I needed to overcome, and at times I didn't think I would survive the five-year stay. All I knew was that I was in Taiwan for a reason and nothing was going to stand in my way. I was determined not to give up."

"Wow! Sounds like you kept going when most would have thrown in the towel," Pistis said.

"I don't know about others, but I was always taught that if there is any way I can do something, and I truly believe it's the right thing to do, I should keep going no matter what," I replied. "That sounds like a great philosophy to live by. Was it ever a challenge for you to decipher what the correct path was?" Pistis asked.

"Yes, sometimes, there were times when I was in a state of complete confusion, yet other times I had absolute clarity about what I needed to do."

"What are things you would do when you found yourself losing focus or becoming confused about what to do?"

"I guess whenever I felt stuck or confused about what to do, I prayed for direction. Plus, I would always try to pay attention to different nudges that I should do something, even if I didn't understand why."

"Like getting the vision to go to Taiwan. What were the nudges like?" Pistis asked, smiling.

"Well, sometimes it was a strong feeling that I should do something. Sometimes it was as if someone was behind me, telling me to do something; a voice that I have come to refer to as 'My Silent Mentor'," I replied with a large smile.

"When is a time when you heard the voice, or as you put it, your 'Silent Mentor'?" Pistis asked.

The flight attendant leaned over and asked Pistis and me if we would like something to drink. Pistis asked for some Sprite and I asked for some orange juice.

"All to Jesus, I surrender, Lord, I give myself to thee; Fill me with Thy love and power, let thy blessings fall on me." – Musixmatch, Words from the song I surrender all. Song writers – Winfield S Weeden & Judson W Van DeVenter

CHAPTER 6:

The Power of a Bun

Thanking the flight attendant, as she served Pistis and me our drinks, I took a sip of orange juice. I then continued my story of listening to what sounded like a voice from behind me, or my silent mentor.

"Ok," I began, "Eli arrived in Taiwan a couple of months after John and I did. Two weeks later, Eli and I met these two girls named May-Lung and Su-Mai. They worked at a hotel in downtown Taipei. One morning after stopping by the hotel to say hi to them, they invited us to go to an outside museum 45 minutes from Taipei, which had a miniature model of Taiwan.

Life was great. We spent the day at the museum and were now on our way back to the hotel with two beautiful girls who were going to treat us to a fancy dinner.

The bus stopped at a stop light, and a voice echoed out as if from someone sitting behind me saying, 'At the next light, get off the bus, go into the Sunrise department store and buy a barbecue pork bun.' Thinking to myself, 'What? Why? I can just get one at the hotel. And besides, I don't even want a barbecue pork bun.' Again, the voice echoed, 'Get off the bus at the next light go into the Sunrise department store and buy a barbecue pork bun.' Now confused and annoyed, I told Eli I couldn't explain why, but I needed to get off the bus and go to the Sunrise department store. But I could meet them at the hotel.

'Why? We can go there later.'

'I can't, I have to do it now. But I can meet you guys later.'

'You know you're crazy right?' Eli replied sharply.

'I don't know how to explain it. But I just got a strong nudge that I have to get off and go there now!'

May-Leung, one of the girls we were with, smiled and said, "My teacher will often say that if you believe for a reason that you can't explain that you really have to do something, then it's because you're being called to do something, but you don't yet know why.

You should go to the store and we can go to the hotel for dinner another time.'

'Really, you two are ok with that?' I asked.

'Yes, but you better hurry or you will miss your stop,' May-Leung said, giggling.

'Thanks, we will call you tomorrow.' Eli and I got up, exited the bus, and walked into The Sunrise department store.

'You owe me big time. They better have food here,' Eli said with a snarl.

Eli and I walked across the store to a large stairwell and headed to the basement where they sold barbecue pork buns. The basement was full of different food stands and in the far corner was a small bakery that sold many different kinds of buns. I remember looking at a clock hanging on the wall. It was 4:50 in the afternoon. As we entered the small bakery, Eli sat down at a small round table and a tall slender girl, who was behind the counter, smiled and asked if she could help me. I then ordered a barbecue pork bun in Cantonese. The girl behind the counter laughed, then told me in English that I had just ordered the bun in Cantonese, but they spoke Mandarin in Taiwan.

I then told her that I could only speak a little bit of Cantonese, and that I still needed to learn Mandarin. The girl then jokingly said, 'You had better go to Hong Kong. They speak Cantonese there.'

'Why don't I teach you English and you teach me Mandarin?' I replied, smiling. We then talked for a few minutes and Eli finally said he was hungry and wanted to get something to eat. He handed the girl a book I was reading and said, 'Here write your phone number down and he can call you tomorrow.'

'Ok, here you go,' The girl said as she wrote down her phone number and handed me the book back. She then wrapped up a couple of buns and handed them to me. We said our goodbyes and left.

I was floating ten feet above the ground. I didn't know how or why but it was as if time came to a standstill. All I could think of was calling the girl back, and the next time I could see her. Eli and I went to a restaurant across the street from where we were staying and had dinner.

'So, what's the deal with the barbecue pork buns? You haven't even eaten them yet,' Eli asked me.

'That's the crazy thing. When I worked at Henry Chang's, if I was upset about something, Henry would give me a barbecue pork bun. It almost became a joke between the two of us. Then, when I was getting ready to leave for Taiwan and stopped by Henry Chang's to say goodbye, Henry gave me a barbecue pork bun and told me that if I ever got home sick to just buy a barbecue pork bun, eat it, and I would feel better. The thing is, today I wasn't homesick or upset. In fact, I couldn't wait to get to the hotel. And even if I was, I could have gotten a barbecue pork bun at the hotel restaurant.' I then told Eli about the voice telling me to get off the bus at the next bus stop and go into the Sunrise department store and buy a barbecue pork bun.

Laughing, Eli said, 'If I didn't know you better, I would think you were crazy. Well at least you got the girl's phone number.'

"So, did you call the girl the next day?" Pistis asked me.

"Yep, that's the craziest part of the whole story. So, the next day I called the girl and we agreed to meet for coffee. A week later we met at a coffee shop, and I found out that she got off work at five o'clock the day we met and that was the last day she worked there. She told me that she started school the next day, so she was glad that I came into the bakery when I did. We became friends, started dating, and finally became engaged four years later. We then married the following next year, which was an amazing experience in its own right," I told Pistis.

"Crazier than the fact that you had a ten-minute window of opportunity to meet your wife?" Pistis asked.

"No, I guess not that crazy, especially since I was on a bus headed to a hotel with Eli and two beautiful girls who were going to treat us to a fancy dinner,' I replied with a large grin.

"Well do tell, how do you go from buying a bun to getting married?" Pistis asked, smiling.

"Shortly after meeting Jennifer, I knew that I wanted to spend the rest of my life with her. Three years later I asked her to marry me."

Jennifer looked at me, smiled, and said, 'Oh no, I'm too young. In a few years I will consider it.'

I truly believed we were meant to be together, and I also knew I needed to be patient and that I couldn't always control the timing, so I needed to have faith that everything would work out. Even though I was saddened by her response, I said okay and changed the subject. A month later, I stopped at her house after teaching an English class. She told me that her father had just called. He told her that he was going to have a party to celebrate his 60th birthday that coming Friday, and that he wanted to announce our engagement at the party. Standing there in a state of shock, I stammered, 'Well, what did you tell him?'

'I told him I would tell you and let him know what you said.'

'Is this what you really want? A month ago, you said you were too young,' I asked.

'I know I'm still young, but I do love you Sam, and now I have my dad's blessing. So yes, this is what I want.'

Still in shock, I said, 'This Friday? That's in only two days. If we get engaged at the party, when will we get married?'

'We could get married the following year,' she explained.

I knew we were meant to be together and that I wanted to marry her, yet I felt a bit like I was on the outside looking in. I had learned years earlier that when things like this happen, often it's through divine intervention. So, it's very important that we learn to listen and follow the signs as they continue to appear to us.

With a big grin on my face, I said, 'Call your dad and tell him yes.' Over the next two days, Jennifer and I bought 200 little engagement cakes to hand out to friends and family. We were married the year after that.

'Why did you buy the little engagement cakes?' Pistis asked.

'Well, in Taiwan the process of becoming engaged, or married for that matter, is quite different than in the US.'

"In which way?"

"It's funny, because in the United States when one becomes engaged, the process tends to be very romantic, and in many ways a private event. You may tell your parents and close friends, but it's really about the couple who was engaged. The guy will ask the girl to marry him or, who knows, the girl may ask the guy to marry her. They then announce the engagement to their closest friends and family. Whereas, in the Chinese culture, it's more of a family affair. Once the couple is about to be engaged and have their parents' permission, they then announce the engagement to immediate family, and more importantly, to extended family and friends, that they are now engaged.

This is done in one of two ways: number one, a large reception will be planned for the couple who is about to become engaged. A day or two before the reception, the couple will deliver small cakes to all of their closest friends and family members, which in our case consisted of delivering 200 little engagement cakes around the neighborhood. Then, the reception is usually held in a restaurant. It can often be almost as large as a wedding reception. Granted, Jennifer's father wanted to announce our engagement at his 60th birthday party, but still there were probably around 200 people there, followed by a 12- course meal.

One year later, we had almost the same sized wedding reception. And, the funny part was that we had to first go to the courthouse and get married in front of a judge to make it legal. Then two weeks later we had the official wedding.

Because of Chinese tradition, it is very important that you get married on a lucky date, and in our case the date that we could get into the courthouse was not a lucky date. However, two weeks later was a very lucky date, so that was the day we had the wedding reception.

We went to the courthouse and got married in front of a judge. However, even though in the eyes of the law we were legally married, we still had to stay in our separate residences because until the marriage was announced and celebrated in front of family and friends, we weren't really married.

I would say there were probably 250 people at the wedding reception, and another 12-course meal. During the reception I only had to wear one suit. However, Jennifer had to wear three different wedding dresses. The reception started with our grand entrance; I was wearing a navy-blue suit and Jennifer wore a long white formal wedding dress. She then changed into a red, very traditional Chinese evening gown. Then, at the end of the reception, Jennifer changed into one more very traditional green formal evening gown, and we stood by the door and thanked everyone for coming. I had a large tray with cigarettes on it and Jennifer had a tray with special wedding candy on it, which people could take as they left.

The funny thing is people talk about how complicated it is to figure out who to invite to a wedding. Because all my family was in the United States, outside of Jennifer's family I only knew six people at my wedding. So, it didn't take much thought or planning on my part. It was kind a like showing up at a dinner party leaving with the best door prize."

"Wow! Sounds like it wasn't what you would have imagined as a child growing up about your wedding someday," Pistis said, chuckling.

"No that it wasn't. Then again neither were most of the experiences I had growing up. Life was never dull - that's for sure."

The heart of a man plans his way, but the Lord establishes his steps. – Proverbs 16:9

"My command is this: Love each other as I have loved you" – John 15:12

CHAPTER 7

Adventures in Taiwan

Another great example of learning to be resilient was when I returned to Taiwan from Hong Kong the time when my visa expired. I only had two months to make enough money to get back into school. So, I had to find a job fast. A friend of mine who taught English in an after-school learning center knew of a class that for some reason, had a really hard time keeping teachers. My friend set up a meeting with the principle who offered to give me a try. She said that if I could control the class, the job was mine.

She then told me that no America teacher ever made it past two lessons, but if I could somehow last, I would have the job for six months. The payment for one month was equal to what most places paid for two months.

'Control the class!' I thought to myself, 'How hard could it be?' We were talking about a class full of middle-school-aged Chinese kids, not a bunch of hoodlums or something. And Chinese kids, from what I could tell, seemed to be well-mannered pleasant kids to be around. All I had to do was connect with these kids and my financial troubles would soon be behind me. No matter what, I was going to keep that job.

I remember walking into the classroom, and the students clearly didn't want me there. They were yelling and carrying on. I stood there in front of the class looking at the students, but they just ignored me. I was beginning to understand why the school couldn't keep teachers in that class. These clearly weren't the well-mannered pleasant kids I had imagined. I couldn't fail. I needed that job. I was down to my last 50 dollars. If I didn't get the job, I would be out of money within two days. The job paid 500 dollars which was enough money to last me for two weeks.

I had to do something, and I had to do it fast. I looked around the room, and in the back of the room there was a large well-built kid sitting in the corner reading a magazine. I looked at him and asked him to come to the front of the class. Looking up at me, he nodded and came up to the front of the class. I reached into my pocket and pulled out my last fifty-dollar bill, saying in Chinese loud enough for everyone to hear,

'I will make you a deal. If you will hit the next kid who talks out of order, makes a noise, or moves loudly in his or her chair as hard as you can, I will give you the fifty dollars. Deal?'

'Really, all I have to do is hit them if they talk and you will give me that fifty dollars?'

'Yep, what do you say?'

'Ok, you have a deal,' He answered back in Chinese.

Amazingly not a sound was heard from a single kid. At the end of the class, the principal came in and sat in the back of the room for a few minutes until I excused the students. She then came up to me and told me that she couldn't believe how well behaved the students were. That somehow, I must have really connected with them and that I had the job if I wanted it.

'That would be great,' I told the school principle, and the next six months things started to take a turn for the better.

I was able to get back into the Chinese school and renew my visa once the two months were up. After six months, I had to once again go back to Hong Kong, but I had enough money by that point, so the trip went pretty well. The best part was that I only had to go there for a day.

I flew to Hong Kong first thing in the morning. I went to a restaurant a friend told me about that served excellent filet mignon and had lunch. Then, I went to a large store there that had all sorts of western food. I bought a bunch of groceries and flew back to Taiwan later that day with two large bags full of peanut butter, jelly, and other American staples. Life was good. I knew that no matter what happened in my life, I could always go to Hong Kong and get a new supply of goodies coupled by amazing filet mignon.

I was starting to feel a little more at home in Taiwan. Yet, no matter how hard I tried, I always felt like I was playing on a field that didn't belong to me. The rules were always changing around me, so I had to continually adapt to each new adventure."

"I find it amazing how you were so confident going across the world and leaving all that you knew behind at such a young age. And, that you weren't terrified by being so far away from home," Pistis said.

"Well granted, part of me was truly terrified at being so far away from home. After all, most of the adults in my life said that I would likely die over there, since I had little money and no way home. Yet, a large part of me knew that as long as I stayed true to my faith, I would always carry God's favor with me. And with His favor, I would never truly be alone.

If I started to second guess myself, or find fear creeping into my life, I would think back to the words out of the hymnal, 'All to Jesus, I surrender, Lord I give myself to thee. Fill me with thy love and power, let they blessings fall on me' that we would sing in the choir back when I was going to Brown Deer Baptist Church. I truly believed my going to Taiwan was for a reason far greater than myself. If that was the case, then who was I to question it."

"Ah yes, 'I Surrender All' – W.S. Weened 1896. That's one of my favorites," Pistis replied.

"I somehow knew that I may have been far from home, but my silent mentor would always be by side."

"And was he?" Pistis asked

"Yes, in ways that I still find it hard to believe. And I was there."

"Still you had such a high level of resilience, or ability to adapt to your surroundings. Did you ever want to just give up and go home?" Pistis asked.

"Yeah, there were many days that I did. However, I didn't really have any choice but to adapt to my surroundings. Life there was anything but stable. And going home never seemed like an option. Speaking of adapting to my surroundings, it's time to shed some of the water I have been drinking. So, I better go visit the bathroom," I replied chuckling.

"You're right, that was some story! Your ability to stay true to that inner voice is really amazing."

"Very true. I don't know why, but I've always been that way as far back as I can remember. I guess that is why I have been able to overcome many of the challenges life has thrown at me," I responded.

"Such as, five years after my arrival, we left Taiwan heading for Milwaukee with what we thought was going to be a two-week layover in Seattle."

"Why did you say you thought you were going to have a two-week layover in Seattle?" Pistis asked.

"At that time, my sister was going to school in Seattle and was going to move back to Milwaukee. So, I told her that Jennifer and I would land in Seattle, visit for a couple of weeks, help load her moving truck and drive it back to Milwaukee. That way, we could help her, and Jennifer could see the country," I answered.

"Something tells me that your plans didn't work out quite as you had expected," Pistis said, chuckling.

"Not exactly. Granted, I did help her load her moving truck and drove it across the country, but it took five years before she was ready to move back to Milwaukee. Jennifer was really busy at work, so she decided to stay in Seattle and work. After moving my sister into her new place, I flew back to Seattle for what was to become a 16-year adventure."

"Wow talk about a detour in your plans. Sure sounds like it was an amazing adventure. That's a great example of this verse, 'The heart of man plans his way, but the Lord establishes His steps' – Proverbs 16:9," Pistis said, laughing.

"Very true, but looking back, the time I was in Taiwan and Seattle allowed me to develop many of the skill sets that I use in my business today. Well, time for a bathroom break!

For he will command his angels concernng you to guard you in all your ways. – Psalm 91:11

Now faith is the substance of things hoped for, the evidence of things not yet seen.
– Hebrews 11:1

CHAPTER 8

Finding One's True Purpose
The transformation of a dream

After returning from the bathroom, I sat down and asked, "Pistis, as people grow in their faith, how do they know if they are on track to finding their true purpose?"

"True faith is believing from a heart level. As it's written in Proverbs 19:2, 'Many are the plans in a person's heart, but it is the Lord's purpose that prevails.' Many people try to intellectually find a solution to a problem or try to explain why something should happen. However, true inspiration or spiritual direction comes to us at the heart level. It doesn't have to necessarily make sense in order for it to be right. It goes back to the core belief, 'Let go, let God'. People often receive guidance from God yet won't give it the credit it deserves.

People will try to live a righteous life, yet one of the greatest ways people fall short of reaching their true greatness is by not living up to their true potential. Now granted at times that can be like walking a tight rope. One person might go through life never really giving it his or her all. Another person might have laser focus, continually striving for excellence, hitting goal after goal. Yet another might have a vision or a dream that's so big society hasn't caught up with it yet. Or, they themselves aren't ready or don't have the necessary skill sets to bring the vision or dream into reality. But they attempt to conquer it anyway; only to fail and give up just short of the finish line," Pistis replied.

"If a person's vision, or dream as you put it, is clear, then I don't see what society has to do with it," I said.

"Ok, let's look at a couple of real-world examples. Bill Gates and Steve Jobs had amazing visions of what computers could do for the average person. True, they brought tremendous resources and designed great companies full of people who helped them bring their visions to life. But still, technology had to be advanced enough, and society had to be open to their ideas in order for them to get the lift or acceptance that they did. If they had tried to accomplish what they did ten years earlier, it would have been far more difficult. Technology was less advanced back then, coupled with the natural rhythm of business that would have blocked their way."

"I guess that makes sense."

"Now, to further prove my point, let's use an example much closer to home. On the plane from Milwaukee to Minneapolis, I asked you about your business and you started to tell me about the business concept you have been working on since you were young. I could sense that deep down you were troubled about your idea as you were talking about it. Then on this flight you told me a little more. It sounds like you are very passionate about your own vision, so what is it about that vision that frustrates you so much?"

"I guess because on one hand, I feel like I have been trying to solve a really large puzzle with many different moving parts. Yet the vision itself is really very simple. I can't help thinking that had I only brought it to life a long time ago, things would be a lot better now not only for me and my family, but for all those I would have been able to help. In many ways, I feel like a failure," I replied, trying to keep from tearing up.

"Sam have you ever watched the transformation of a caterpillar into a butterfly?"

"Yes, I found a caterpillar when I was young and kept it in a jar until it turned into butterfly."

"Ok, let's say that back then you decided the world needed more butterflies, so you opened the jar, took a knife, and cut open the cocoon that was protecting the caterpillar during the transformation period. That way the butterfly could be released and enter the world even faster. What would have happened?"

"That's silly. If I did that the caterpillar would die and the transformation would never happen."

"I see, now let's say you waited until one week before the transformation was finished and cut the cocoon open. Would you be able to speed up the transformation so that the world could enjoy the butterfly's beauty?"

"First of all, there is no way I would know the timing, but assuming I was able to know when the transformation process was almost finished, if you cut the cocoon open, and by some miracle the butterfly didn't die, it would probably be missing a wing or something. So why not wait just one more week?"

"So, it would be safe to say that outside of having some kind of machine that could track the transformation process, only God would know such detail?"

So too is it Sam, with God's timing for your vision. You have been looking at your vision much like the butterfly and trying to find ways to prematurely cut it out of its cocoon. Like the transformation of the caterpillar into a butterfly, your dream enterprise needs to follow its own transformation process. Like the butterfly, only God knows the true timing.

Crying to God in frustration because your business isn't growing as fast as you would like is the same as crying out to God because your butterfly is still stuck inside of its cocoon waiting to hatch! I would suggest that you thank God for giving you such a large vision that it forces you to continually grow outside your comfort zone. And, for a vision that is so profound that it's taking so long for it to transform into the business you visualize."

"I just get so frustrated because I keep working on the business and it still looks the same. When will it be ready to thrive?"

"Sam, have you ever considered that you keep looking at your vision in many similar ways to how you watched the caterpillar turn into a butterfly as a child? Rather, I would argue that you are the caterpillar transforming into the butterfly. And your dream enterprise is the brilliance that resonates from you similar to the beauty of the butterfly.

It's time for you to really let go and let God truly guide you. Do you honestly believe you were ready to start your dream business, as you put it, back then?" Pistis asked.

"I don't know. I knew how to start and build a business, and I systematized the referral system I was using in the limousine business. I was even teaching the process to others."

"Was there already someone doing what your dream business would do, someone you could have followed?"

"No that's what's so frustrating. Given the scope of what my vision was, there weren't really any examples; at least within the framework of my vision. I would have been first to market," I replied.

"That may have been the case, but still even the best idea has a season for which it will flourish. Like my earlier example, if it's not the right time for an idea, no matter how inspired a person is by the idea, it will fail. For an idea to be fully successful, there are three key things that must first take place. First, there has to be a need for it in the marketplace. Second, the innovator must have the necessary capital and know how to bring the idea to life. Third, there needs to be the appropriate people and resources in place to help bring the idea to fruition. Did you have these three components in place even ten years ago?"

"Well, there was the market for the idea ten years ago, but I didn't have the necessary funds or people around me that could have helped me bring it to life."

"Ok, so even though there was a market for your idea, you didn't have the money at the time to properly do it?" Pistis asked.

"To do it properly? No! But I could have started with limited capital and built it from there," I replied.

"And how has that worked for you with other projects you have done?"

"Not very well, but those were different."

"I see, those were different. And why's that?"

"Because the business I envisioned could have helped many different people get their businesses off the ground," I answered.

"Ok, do me a favor. Close your eyes and let's travel back to 2006. What does your average day look like?" Pistis said.

"We had just moved to Milwaukee from Seattle, and I was working as the director of training for RE/MAX. I spent quite a bit of my day creating training programs and trying to recruit new agents. Plus, I was really involved in the kids' school," I said.

"Ok, now give me a recap of your dream business. What would it have looked like?" Pistis asked.

"Well, it would have served as a business incubator designed to create a supportive environment for like-minded professionals and entrepreneurs working together in a dynamic member-based community. As the member's businesses continue to grow, they would be able to serve their clients at a much deeper level.

The goal of the community would be to continually help our members grow their business through creating consistent referrals from their databases. Thereby, allowing them to truly serve their customers and clients while creating a consistent income.

The incubator would also provide a combination of continued support, training, great tools, and core business resources. I have always believed that people are created to reach great heights. However, first they must feel safe, supported, encouraged, and guided through the process. By ourselves we can do great things, yet together we can climb the highest mountains. I honestly don't know why it's taken me so long to finish it."

"Wow it sounds like a very lofty goal. But it also sounds like a business that will take a fair amount of working capital to build it properly," Pistis said smiling.

"Yeah, I guess you're right, which also frustrates me. I have been doing so many things since 2006, yet none of them have made very much money. Given my skill sets, I should have made a lot more money. I feel like I have been struggling just to get by," I said, letting out a long sigh while shaking my head.

"And why do you think that is?" Pistis asked.

"I don't know, sometimes I think we should have just stayed in Seattle."

"Ok, fair enough, remember though; all the skill in the world isn't enough. Your income will only grow to the level of your own self esteem. Let's explore that for a moment. On the flight to Minneapolis, you told me that you moved back to Milwaukee so that you could be closer to your family. Would it also be fair to say you believed that God was calling you in that direction?"

Confused by how he could possibly know that, I paused then answered, "Yes."

"You have a strange look on your face, as if there is more to the story," Pistis said smiling.

"Ok, so I told you about how I sold the limousine company and we moved back to Milwaukee in 2005. Well, the rest of the story as they say is I turned 40 in October that year, and we went back to Milwaukee to visit during Christmas vacation. The whole time we were in Milwaukee, I really felt like we should move back so that we could be closer to my mom and dad. Jennifer was still really busy with her job and Newcastle Limousine was finally successful, so moving back to Milwaukee didn't make any sense. We flew back to Seattle and life continued as usual, except the feeling that we were supposed to move back to Milwaukee kept growing stronger and stronger.

One morning, I woke up with tears running down my face as I had this really strong nudge that we were supposed to be in Milwaukee. I started to pray about it and the feeling kept getting stronger. I told Jennifer over breakfast one morning that I didn't understand why, but I truly felt like God was calling us back to Milwaukee.

She looked at me like I just told her that I thought we should move to the moon. 'You feel like God is calling us back to Milwaukee?' She repeated.

'Yes, I'm not sure if it's because my mom's health isn't very good at the moment? I know it doesn't make any sense, but I keep getting these strong nudges that it's time for us to move back,' I answered.

'If I thought it would make any difference, I would tell you that I think you're crazy. But I know you and your nudges. So, you think God is calling us to pick up, leave everything we have worked so hard to create, and move back to Milwaukee?'

'That's correct.'

'And, if it's truly God's divine intervention, then it all should smoothly work out, right?'

'I would think so.'

'Ok, you have 30 days from today to figure everything out and make it happen. But I don't want to move until the kids are out of school for the summer,' Jennifer replied with a deep sigh.

'What do you mean by figure everything out?' I asked.

'I mean you have to find a buyer for Newcastle Limousine since you can't run it from Milwaukee, find a buyer for our house here, and find a new house in Milwaukee for us to move into. We need a house that is close to your mom, yet in a school district that is better than the one we are in here. Oh, and I need to get my boss to let me work from Milwaukee,' she said.

'Well, I did quite a bit of research and I think we can get $550,000 for this house, so we should be able to find a decent house back there for what we will have left over after paying all the closing costs.'

'What only $550,000? No way! I want at least $600,000 otherwise I don't want to sell this house,' she responded.

'Seriously, there is no way we can get $600,000 for this house in this market, especially in only 30 days!' I snapped back.

'I thought you told me it was divine intervention. You believed God was calling us to move back to Milwaukee!' Jennifer snapped back.

'I truly believe that, but ...'

'But what? Who are you to second guess God? If it's truly divine intervention as you put it, then there is no reason why you can't find a buyer who's willing to pay $600,000 for this house, even in this market, find a buyer for your limousine company, and find a great house near your mom's in thirty days,' Jennifer exclaimed as she got up and left the room.

I just sat there in complete confusion. What had just happened, and why? The last thing I wanted to do was sell Newcastle Limousine. It was finally doing really well. It was consistently earning a profit. I really liked many of my clients and loved running the company. Plus, because we needed a place to park our limousines, we bought a small house on an acre lot. A short time after we moved into the house, a property developer who I worked with at the real estate firm I was with was developing the lot next to us and building five houses on it.

He suggested that if I also develop our lot while living there, I would be able to build three new houses, remodel our house, and build a large garage to store the limousines. Plus, we would likely be able to net around a million dollars. Now I was supposed to walk away from it all, move to Milwaukee and start over. I just sat there with tears running down my cheeks.

Then again Jennifer was right, who was I to second guess God? If moving to Milwaukee truly was His desire, then it would all come together. Closing my eyes, I prayed to God asking Him to continue to guide me and give me the strength to become the leader, father, and husband He designed me to be."

"And did it all smoothly come together?" Pistis asked, with an even bigger smile.

"Yep, I put our house on the market for $600,000 and we received a full-price offer with the new buyers agreeing to let us rent it back from them until the kids got out of school for summer vacation. One of the larger limousine companies I worked with happily bought Newcastle Limousine, as they wanted our corporate client base and our marketing system.

I flew back to Milwaukee, found and wrote an offer on a house in Whitefish Bay, (a suburb just north of Milwaukee) which was known for having the best school district in the area and was only ten minutes from my mom's house. However, as I was getting back on the plane to return to Seattle, I found out that the house in Whitefish Bay had just sold. I sat there in a state of shock. Things had been moving along perfectly. Now what? I didn't have time to go back to Milwaukee and find another house. So, I just put my head down and said, 'Ok God, you know what's best for us. I will continue do my part, so please help me find a great house.'

The plane landed back in Seattle and there was a message on my phone to call the real estate agent back in Milwaukee right away. I got off the plane and called the agent.

'Mike you're not going to believe this, but an hour after you and I hung up the phone. I got a call from the other buyer's agent saying that the buyers were walking away from the deal because the chimney needs to be rebuilt, even though the sellers were willing to fix and pay the full cost to have it done. And, the best part was that because the sellers had to rebuild the chimney, they wouldn't be able to close until July 5th, which turned out to be 5 days after we had to move out of our current house. Finally, Jennifer's boss agreed to let her work from Wisconsin since most of what she did was over the internet anyway. I couldn't have planned it better if I tried. Everything worked out perfectly down to the last detail," I said, with a big smile on my face.

"That's some story," Pistis said, laughing.

"Yeah, I guess it is," I agreed.

"So then, Sam if it was by God's will, or calling as you put it, that you were able to move your family back to Milwaukee and you wanted to live your life by trying to stay true to that will, how could things possibly have been anything different?"

"You make a very good point. I guess I just wonder why, if it really was God's will, am I still struggling so much. I feel like my business, should be further along than it is. Would my business and family be better off if we had stayed in Seattle?"

"Just for the sake of argument, let's pretend that you never moved back to Milwaukee and everything stayed on track. What do you suppose that would have looked like?" Pistis suggested.

"Well, Jennifer would have continued to work at her job. The kids would have continued to go to their school. Although, Sabrina would have had to move to a different school; one probably not as good. I would have continued to grow Newcastle Limousine and we would have continued to develop the property. In fact, we needed to start the construction work on the property by the end of 2006 and probably would have just finished building one - maybe two - of the houses that we were going to put on the property by the end of 2008."

"Would you have been able to still live there while you were doing all of this?"

"No, we probably would have had to buy another house while we finished the construction project."

"Sounds like you would have been heavily leveraged in mortgages, between your new house and the construction project itself. Did you have enough extra money coming in from either limousine company or Jennifer's job, to cover any short falls?"

"No, that was the scary part; we were barely scraping by as it was."

"So, life could have been very exciting, or very scary. In fact, circumstances could have gone from good to bad very quickly if things hadn't gone as planned," Pistis said with a grin.

"Yeah, I guess that's true."

"Ok then, back to our walk down memory lane. Do you remember what happened to the economy in 2007 and 2008?"

"Yes, in 2007 the real estate market crashed and in 2008 the stock market crashed. The overall economy slid into a deep recession," I answered.

"So, if everything remained status quo, you would have bought another house probably with a relatively high mortgage. You would have had for sure one, but probably two, brand new homes to sell with very high construction loans on them in a market where no one would be able to buy them. Plus, as I recall, because of the deep recession, two-thirds of the limousine companies in Seattle went out of business."

"Funny you should say that because I just found out two weeks ago from the person I sold New Castle Limousine to, that two of the companies I did a lot of work with went out of business. Macy's, one of our largest accounts, moved their headquarters to California, which meant that I would have most likely lost our biggest accounts," I said, shaking my head.

"Sounds like a quick trip to bankruptcy if you ask me, even for someone who had a fair amount of working capital to work with. And, as you put it you were just scraping by - your cash flow was running pretty lean. If you had tried to start your dream business then, it probably would have never made it out of the starting gate. Would you agree with me?"

"Yeah, I guess that's true," I replied, with a surprised look on my face.

"Still think following your nudge, God's guidance, and moving your family to Milwaukee was a bad choice?" Pistis

The asked with a light chuckle.

"Wow! I guess I never really looked at it like that," I replied.

"Yeah, I find that very few people ever think their outcomes completely through, carefully weighing all the different possibilities for how it could have turned out. They then get mad and blame God, when in fact He was there guiding them all along," Pistis said.

"Ok then, how about now? What will it take to build your dream business now?"

"I guess I still need to raise the money, plus I need to find people who can help."

"Do you truly believe that the inspiration for your business came from God?"

Yes, that's why it's so frustrating it's taking so long to launch it."

"Well, do you know enough to build your dream business now?"

"Yes."

"Is there a need for what you want to do now?"

"Yes, now more the ever."

"Do you have enough capital to at least launch it on a limited basis?"

"Yes, if I start small and slowly build it. But I still need to find people who can help."

"Wouldn't it be fair to say then, that if your dream business is truly part of your life's purpose, God will bring people into your life who can help you build it?"

"Yeah, I have already seen His continued intervention and guidance in building out the foundation for the business."

"Really, like how?" Pistis asked.

"I guess in a way, ever since I was a teenager, I have been able to sow the seeds for my dream or business plan. Over the five years I was in Taiwan, besides meeting Jennifer, I was able to meet and learn from many different mentors. When I was in Taiwan, I would often journal about the trip, my business plan, and I created my very first dream board there.

I knew shortly after landing in Seattle, there were things I needed to learn there before I would be ready to return home.

It also seemed like a great place for Jennifer to begin her journey in America. I just didn't know how long it would take. And, the limousine company I had started became a great classroom for learning how to build a business. Plus, I talked to and learned from many of my clients over the years.

I would keep plugging away, trying to put all the different building blocks together for the business' foundation. When I seemed to reach a road block, I would cry out to God for guidance and He would open the next door I needed to walk through.

I remember one such time; we had moved back to Milwaukee and it was becoming more and more clear that I had learned what I needed to from real estate, and it was time to leave RE/MAX. I kept being drawn towards the need for a financial advising or planning component to my plan.

When Sabrina was eight, she came home from school one day and told me she wanted to design a business that would teach money management skills to children. I had a strong feeling that her business would become an important part of my vision. I just didn't know how. Since then, Sabrina and I have continued to teach children and their parents how to develop a proactive money management system.

Our biggest challenge, however, was that we knew once they mastered the basics, they needed a trusted financial advisor who would help them create a comprehensive financial plan designed around their dreams and goals, and then continue to work with them through the process. I had interviewed various people in the financial industry and found that even though there are a lot of great advisors out there, unless a person had a considerable amount of money, it was hard to get the ongoing personal attention that I believed people just starting out needed.

I often thought about getting my financial licenses, so I could better serve our clients, and even interviewed with a couple of different financial firms.

However, they never seemed like the right fit. I knew that finding the right mix of financial solutions and the business philosophy of creating long-term client-focused relationships was very important. I knew that until I found the right firm, it would continue to be a large missing link in my plan.

Knowing that the right firm would appear when the time was right, I studied as much as I could about business and finances. Sabrina and I kept doing seminars teaching children and their parents the discipline necessary for developing healthy money management habits. At night when the kids were asleep, I worked on my vision and the business plan, continually perfecting and expending on the vision.

One evening, after a couple of really hard months of soul searching, I dropped to my knees in frustration and called out in prayer, 'Please God, if I'm on the wrong path then tell me what to do, and I'll do it. But if I am supposed to continue working on my vision, and if that vision is to be geared around helping children, parents, and small business owners develop a solid financial and business foundation, then please please open a door for that to happen.'

The next morning, I was supposed to give a speech for Toastmasters on goal setting. But at the last minute, I had a strong feeling that I needed to talk about becoming financially independent instead. I changed my speech at the very last minute. Having only five minutes to redo my speech, I put my speech on goal setting down, got up and spoke from the heart.

After Toastmasters was over, one of the members of the club came up to me and said he was really impressed by my passion about helping people get their finances in order. He then asked,

if I was in the financial business.

I said, 'No, but I often think about it.'

He then told me he was really busy at work and that he wasn't planning to go to Toastmasters that morning, but had a strong feeling at the last minute that he needed to be there. So, he jumped in the car and went.

After hearing my speech, he knew why he needed to be there. He then told me they were having an open house at his office and he would like to invite me. That night I went to his office, and for the first time in many years I had this overwhelming feeling that I was home.

I didn't understand why, but everything felt so comfortable, as if I had been there before. A week later, after joining the firm, I was leaving an appointment I had about a mile from the office. As I left the appointment, I made a left turn and started up a hill to the road that went back to the office. I pulled over in amazement. There it was right in front of me: my dad's old house. Tears streamed down my face as I sat there. Memory after memory resurfaced as if they were on fast forward.

Wiping the tears away from my face, I reached down, picked up my phone, and dialed my dad's number. 'Hello,' my dad answered.

'Hi dad it's me, I'm sitting in front of the Grandville house, and I just wanted to say how sorry I am for being such a punk back then.'

'Hey kiddo, don't worry about it. You were just being a normal fifteen-year-old kid, stuck in a situation you didn't want to be in. I'm sorry too, for not being there when you needed me.'

We talked for a while and after we hung up, I felt this incredible sense of peace come over me.

I started to laugh, as I realized that the office was on Grandview drive, one mile away from my dad's old house. I developed a friendship with a guy in the firm who lived just around the corner from where my dad had lived. Is it just a small world or …?"

"Do you really need me to answer that?" Pistis said, laughing.

"I remember the night my mom and I went back to my dad's house to get my stuff. As I left his front yard and got into my mom's car, I told myself that someday I would return and make things right. Then, the morning I was at Elmbrook listening to Stuart Briscoe give his sermon on God's grace, the anchor was laid. My dad and I didn't talk for a year or two after that. Later that fall, he sold his house and moved to Indiana. For years, I never thought about Grandville drive, yet the anchor was still there in the background waiting to resurface until the night I went to the open house at the financial firm, which made joining the firm a very natural move. The reason for our moving back to Milwaukee was right there in front of me. I was now in the financial business, and I was on my way to completing the final stage of the dream I've been working on all those years.

Chris my friend from Toastmasters, and two of the leaders in the office, had become great mentors. I was convinced that meeting them was the reason for our moving back to Milwaukee when we did. I hoped that if I continued to grow myself and build a strong business, everything would fall into place at the right time.

I knew that together we could accomplish amazing things, but change would have to occur first. At a point when I once again started to question if I was on the right path, my mentors shared with us their own challenges, and that they had also been looking for a better way. It became crystal clear why I met them, and that they held the key to the final stage in implementing my dream. That in fact, we shared very similar dreams.

That night, they announced that they were going to create a financial firm that was completely independent from outside influences, so it could put the client's needs first always; a firm designed to make a radical difference in the way financial planning is done."

"Wow, that's a great example of staying true to your faith. The challenge is that believing in something that strongly, or having pure faith, requires total loyalty; even when all else seems impossible. Most people unfortunately forget to pay attention to the signs in front of them, as obvious as they may be."

"It has definitely taken its toll though at times. Over the years, my life has moved in many different directions. Often times, those who were close to me felt like I was living in my own sense of reality. And many times, they were probably right. It was as if I had an inner compass leading me from one journey to another. As long as I stayed focused on my dream, one door would shut closing out that chapter, and another one would open. The hard part was that even though I saw the new door that had just opened, to those around me, there was nothing there. It was business as usual. So, I would make a change in what I was doing, or decide to go somewhere else, and it wouldn't make any sense to those around me.

I often looked like I was about to walk off a cliff, figuratively anyway. I have always been driven by an inner sense of faith that in the end everything will turn out as planned. Even when things hit a roadblock, I knew a door would open and the answer would show itself. I just needed to remain patient and keep looking out for it. It has been because of that faith that I have been able to stay on track with my dream over all these years.

With each new change God put in front of me, I always had the mentors needed at that point in time to move my vision forward. I often felt like I was putting together a large puzzle, and with each passing week, month, and year the different pieces of the puzzle would be revealed to me. Every now and then something would happen that would change my course of direction, yet the dream always stayed out in front. The vision I had when I was a child became more and more clear, yet still had missing components to it."

"As I sit here listening to you, two things come to mind. First, you have an amazing internal compass, and the fact you're willing to follow it like you do even when others may think you're crazy, is very unique. And second, it's clear that given the scope of your dream business, and the degree to which your business will bless many lives as you continue to design it, it's going to take a community much larger than yourself. So, remain patient and trust that God will continue to guide you as long as you continue to do all that you can and remain a faithful servant. There is no reason to feel frustrated that it's taking too long. Just like you told your daughter when she was at MYSO, you can't always control the timing, just your activities. If you perform the necessary activities and continue to go to God through prayer, then the results will come in God's timing. As one of my favorite verses goes,

'The mind of man plans his way. But the Lord directs his steps' – Proverbs 16:9," Pistis said with a large smile.

"True you have definitely been on a unique path. The question is why, and how are you going to apply what you have learned to your life? Those are questions put in front of most, if not all, people at different times in their lives. The challenge is that most people ignore the signs. Yet, for some reason, you didn't."

"Yeah, it appears so, but not always by my own choice I might add."

"Not by your own choice! What do you mean by that? How can anyone force you to do something, outside of using brute force to do so?" Pistis asked.

"Well, it may not have been by brute force, but I have found that life has a way of throwing challenges into our lives when we least expect it, and definitely don't deserve such challenges, which has been a bone of contention of mine for some time now," I answered.

"You're not alone; most people feel the same way. That's why so many people face life from an angry or fearful state. People want to feel confident in their day-to-day actions, and when they don't, they either get mad, become fearful, or lean into their inner faith that things will work out in the end," Pistis said.

"That makes sense. I too have felt all three emotions many times throughout my life," I replied.

"Exactly. So, if you, even with your strong faith, often fall into that trap, it's no wonder that most other people do as well."

"True, but it seems like there should be an easier way."

"There is, but most people aren't willing to surrender the degree of control needed in order to experience that level of faith. First, one must have complete and absolute faith; then they will be ready to surrender the feeling of total control.

Life is a gradual flux of energy. Everyone plays into that core essence of energy, both good and bad. The ultimate question is do people contribute positive or negative energy to the mix? Unfortunately, it's a give and take. If there is more positive energy flowing into life, then growth happens. If there is more negative energy flowing into the mix, then apathy will take over.

That's why it's so important that we always try our best to stay positive and hopeful even when things feel out of control. There are seasons in life when one experiences happiness, sadness, anger, and fear. The ultimate question is are we in control of our emotions, or controlled by them? If we find ourselves in a season of sadness, it's important to allow and pay attention to those feelings both through prayer and talking about what caused the sadness with someone who can help guide us through the healing process."

"So, if I understand you correctly Pistis, we as members of a community, are responsible for the overall essence of our culture depending on the degree to which our own energy is at. And that's why it's so important for people to set goals and continually strive for peace and balance for a better life. Is this why it's so important for us to learn to lean into a power higher than ourselves?"

"That's correct Sam. If we always try to do everything ourselves, we will fall short because of our own limitations."

"I guess I understand what you mean; like when I first decided to go to Taiwan. The decision to go to Taiwan was very exciting, yet very scary. I knew that only bringing one hundred dollars with me was somewhat risky. I would quickly run out of money. If that wasn't bad enough, everyone I shared my plan with told me I was crazy and would most likely die over there. And then, to think that I was supposed to remain there for five years! What was I thinking? I could only speak a little Cantonese, and in Taiwan they speak Mandarin. Here I was about to get on a plane, fly half-way across the world, get off the plane in a land that speaks a completely different language than I could speak, and I had no way home! Thinking back, sometimes I think I must have been crazy for going at such a young age."

"I bet many people probably thought so too. It's amazing that you even considered it," Pistis said, laughing.

Just then the flight attendant came by with another basket full of snacks. Pistis grabbed a bag with miniature brownie pieces in it. I grabbed another cookie, and to my surprise this time the flight attendant had sea salt chocolate caramels in the basket. I took one, telling the flight attendant that my daughter loved them, and asked if I could have another one for her.

"But of course," she said, smiling.

"What were some other adventures you had and lessons you learned while in Taiwan?" Pistis asked

Just as I was getting ready to answer Pistis, the flight attendant returned with a small sandwich bag full of the sea salt chocolate caramels. "Here you go Mr. Raber, I hope your daughter enjoys them," she said as she handed them to me.

Thanking the flight attendant, I told her that giving the sea salt chocolate caramels to my daughter was a great example of why I enjoy flying Delta so much. I am always amazed at how well they take care of their passengers.

"You're welcome and thanks again for flying with us and for your continued loyalty," she replied.

There is a time for everything, and a season for every activity under the Heavens: - Ecclesiastes 3:1

CHAPTER 10

The Law of the Talents

"One of the key lessons I learned growing up was that no matter what happens, I had to continue to search for the true reason behind what was happening to me. Like going to Taiwan. Sure, I wanted to open a Chinese restaurant. And, the fact that Henry Chang would help me open one if only I could survive there for five years was great. Yet I still somehow knew that God had an even higher purpose for why I was there, and it was up to me to search for that reason.

The thing that has puzzled me for many years was that even though I have been in search of what that purpose is for most of my life, it seemed like many people are either content with whatever life brings them or they feel frustrated, but still don't put a lot of effort in trying to find out what that higher purpose is," I said to Pistis.

"True, it may look like that on the surface. For most people, the challenge comes in how to reach that higher purpose, or even what that purpose is if there is one. Even for you, as you said you have been searching for that purpose for most of your life, and you are a lot closer to that source then most. So, if it's that difficult for *you* to stay on track, you can imagine how hard it would be for someone who had never heard about or thought of such a purpose even existing," Pistis answered.

"How is it that you seem to know me better then I know myself?" I asked

"How is it that you do not? You're always examining yourself," Pistis answered.

"I don't know. I guess it goes back to my question about finding my purpose," I said.

"Maybe it's because most people, including you, think of finding one's purpose as if it's some island out in the middle of the ocean. People want a map, or someone to show them where that purpose is. One's purpose isn't a destination; it's a journey of becoming who you were designed to be. If I were to tell you where or what your purpose is right now, it would be like telling an eight-month-old baby how to walk.

You could draw fancy diagrams or step-by-step instructions on how to first sit up, then how to crawl, get up, and start walking. But that child is going to fall down just the same. It might even take the child another six months before he or she actually walks.

Your purpose is the same. You have to grow into the person you were designed to be, and from that you are able to fully live your life designed around your purpose. Once again, finding your purpose is a journey not a destination. We are all born with different talents, and those talents make following our purposes easier. However, we first have to fine tune those talents like an eight-month-old baby has to strengthen his or her legs before standing."

"So, if I understand you correctly, the first step is to discover what our talents are, then figure out how we can best use those talents to help those around us or serve our community," I said.

"Yes, by discovering what your God-given talents are, you will be better able to help yourself grow into the person you were designed to be. From there you will be able to help those around you, connecting you to your purpose," Pistis explained.

"I see, so it goes back to becoming the best I can be."

"Correct. Are you familiar with the parable 'The Law of the Talents'?" Pistis asked.

Yes, it's the story of the rich man who was leaving town and gave a talent, or piece of gold, to three servants to hold on to for him. Correct?" I said.

"Yes, but let me spin it another way. What if Matthew wasn't talking about gold, rather he was talking about people's God-given talent or abilities?" Pistis asked.

"Interesting. I guess I always looked at it as the rich man was giving the servants talents or pieces of gold," I said.

"I'm going to say the parable again, but this time listen as if instead of gold, I'm talking about one's God-given talents," Pistis said.

"Matthew 13:3-8 'And he spoke many things unto them in parables. Saying, behold, a sower went forth to sow; and when he sowed, some seeds fell by the wayside, and the fowls came and devoured them up. Some fell upon stony places, where they had not much earth, and forthwith they sprung up, because they had no deepness of earth; and when the sun was up, they were scorched; and because they had no root, they withered away.

And some fell among thorns; and the thorns sprung up and choked them; But others fell into good ground and brought forth fruit; Some a hundredfold; Some sixtyfold; Some thirtyfold.

A wise man was traveling to a faraway country. He called forth three servants, and to one he gave five talents, to another he gave two, and to another he gave one. To each according to his own ability; and immediately he went on a long journey.

Then he who had five talents went and traded with them and made another five talents. And likewise, he who had received two gained two more also. But he who had received one went and dug a hole in the ground and put his talent in it. After a long time, the master of those servants returned to settle accounts with them.

The one who had five talents came and brought five more with him, Lord you gave me five talents, look I have gained five more besides them. His lord said to him, well done, good and faithful servant. You have been faithful over a few things. I shall make you ruler over many things. Enter into the joy of your Lord.

The one who had received two talents said; Lord you gave me two talents, look I have gained two more besides them. His lord said to him, well done, good and faithful servant. You have been faithful over a few things I shall make you ruler over many things. Enter into the joy of your Lord.

Then he who had received the one talent came and said to the Lord, I know you to be a hard man, reaping where you have not sown, and gathering where you have not scattered seed. And I was afraid and went and hid the talent in the ground. Look, here you have what is yours.

But his Lord answered and said to him, you wicked and lazy servant. You knew that I reap where I have not sown and gather where I have not scattered seed. So, you ought to have deposited my money with the bankers, and at my coming I would have received back my own with interest. So, take the talent from him and give it him who has ten talents. For it is to everyone who has more, more will be given. And he will have abundance. But him who does not have, even what he has will be taken from away. And cast the unprofitable servant into the outer darkness.'

Many will say that this parable is talking about money. I would again beg to argue that it is actually talking about our God-given purpose or gifts. We are all born with different talents and some make full use of them, yet many others never live up to their potential. That is why along the journey of finding our true purpose for life, it's so important to be on an on-going quest to grow ourselves.

People are all different. Some are born with great abilities, and some are born with abilities that don't appear to be that great; what someone might even call average or below average. All people are born in the image of God; therefore all people are born with God-given abilities that are equally important as a whole.

One might look at the guy pushing a broom and say but he's only a janitor. They forget that the janitor may be a wonderful father with small children at home waiting to be fed with the money he makes pushing that broom. Or they forget that they like walking on clean floors, yet they aren't willing to pick up a broom. So, the janitor did them a great service by cleaning the floor so they have a clean floor to walk on.

Our different talents and abilities are what allow us to live in a great community. It's up to us to continually grow and finetune those abilities on our journeys toward finding our purpose, then serving that purpose to the best of our abilities. Or put another way, 'Your talent is God's gift to you. What you do with it, is your gift back to God' - Leo Buscaglia."

If any of you lacks wisdom, let him ask God, who gives generously to all without reproach, and it will be given him. - James 1:5

Do not be anxious about anything, but in every situation, by prayer and petition, with thanksgiving, present your requests to God - Philippians 4:6

CHAPTER 12

Let Go - Let God

The pilot once again came over the intercom and announced that we were beginning our descent into Seattle. He asked the flight attendants to prepare the cabin for landing.

"Wow, we are almost to Seattle. Time flew by fast! In the short time we have left, tell me what you think your largest struggle has been as you have continued through your journey," Pistis said.

"Wow, my largest struggle? I guess it would be low self-confidence. Growing up, a lot of the people I looked up to tended to be very negative and often criticized the things I was doing. Or, they continually put down things that I cared about and that were part of who I was as a person."

"What do you mean by who you were as a person?" Pistis asked.

"Like when I lived in the house with my mom after moving out of John's house. I was the only male in the house, and the women who lived there felt entitled to slam men and talk about how awful they were every chance they got.

Many times, after being around the other people in the house, I would get up and go to my room and just sit there looking out of my bedroom window wondering why John chose Hawaii and being with the counter girl over me. I would ask myself; 'What did I do wrong to cause John to want to go so far away?'

At times, I sat in my room and it seemed like the world was closing in on top of me. Sometimes I found it awfully hard to breath. I knew I needed to get up and go outside, yet I really wanted to climb under a rock somewhere."

"Sounds like a tough place for a young boy to be around," Pistis replied.

"Yeah, my self-confidence sure took a hit because of it. For years I believed that I had low self-confidence or an inferiority complex; that I was somehow subpar to those around me. For years I faced down the many dragons, or life's challenges, without ever looking back. Yet, when it came to business, I couldn't close the

the simplest of transactions. I would wonder why I was firing on only two cylinders, instead of four. Was I lacking in the necessary skill sets to get the job done?"

"What is confidence or lack of confidence anyway? Many people like to equate it with an inferiority complex; the fear of not being good enough to deserve ultimate victory. People doubt their self-worth or compare themselves to those around them instead of being proud of whom God designed them to be. People are made in the image of God, so as long as they stay true to their God-given purpose, then they should be confident that true victory will come to them regardless of what someone else might say. In the end, only God's judgment truly matters. Why do you suppose that your self-confidence was so low, when you have always had the heart of a champion?" Pistis asked.

"I guess it was because for most of my life, no matter what I accomplished it seemed to never be good enough for those I looked up to. I would watch people around me and all their accomplishments and was always in awe at how easy it seemed for them. Now, logic would tell me that they had to work hard for that success. But I worked hard. Why wasn't I experiencing such success? The problem was, I was so busy comparing myself to others that I never stopped to wonder what others might think when looking at me," I replied, shaking my head.

"If people are made in the image of God, then wouldn't it only make sense that people strive to become the best versions of themselves that they can be - the best version of *themselves*, being the important part? Not the best version of someone else. If we strive to live our lives according to our God-given purpose, then comparing oursselves to others cheapens the greatness that exists in each and every one of us," Pistis said.

"In a way, it's been interesting because John tried to instill physical confidence in me, and my dad tried to instill spiritual confidence in me. They both came in and out of my life at different times and in many ways. Yet, they were taken out of my life while I still had many questions for them.

I guess I felt abandoned by them both: first by my dad l when I was little, then by John going off to Hawaii; and then again by my dad when I had to move back in with my mom at age fifteen. Somehow something always seemed to be missing. Maybe that's why it was so hard to say good-bye to my dad the last time I saw him."

"What do you mean the last time you saw him?"

"Well, two summers ago after dropping Sam off at a camp, Monica and I drove 450 miles out of our way instead of driving straight home so we could stop by and see my dad. I had a strong feeling that I needed to see him.

You see, my dad had pancreatic cancer. After a long day of driving, Monica and I pulled up in front of my dad's house. He was in front of his house cutting the grass. Rolling the window down I yelled out to my dad, 'Hey should you be cutting the grass?'

Smiling, he yelled back, 'Why not? I feel great - a little tired - but otherwise great! However, I sure am hungry.' Laughing, he then said, 'I am glad to see you, but what are you doing here?'

'We thought it would be nice to see you. Plus, I figured the grass probably needed cutting. Do you want to go get something to eat?' I asked.

'Why not?' my dad said as he got into our car. We drove down the hill to a restaurant he really liked and had dinner.

After dinner, my dad gave me a big hug and said that he sure was glad we came, but that there was plenty of time to see each other; that we didn't need to drive 450 miles out of our way just to have dinner with him. I smiled and said, 'Actually I came to help you cut the grass, and dinner was an added perk.'

Two weeks later the phone rang. It was Carol telling us that dad had taken a turn for the worse, and that we should come as soon as possible. We quickly gathered our stuff, jumped in the car, and headed towards the hospital.

We arrived later that day and sat next to his bed as he slept. 30 minutes or so later, he woke up and smiled as he saw us sitting there. We talked and laughed together as the hours rolled by.

Around 8:00pm he said that he was tired and wanted to take a nap.

We got our stuff together, stood up, and said we were going to head home so he could rest, but would be back the next weekend to check in on him.

Leaning over him, I gave him a big hug, fighting back tears as I said, 'Rest now and I will see you soon dad.'

'Ok, see you soon son,' he replied.

We left, got in the car, and headed back to Milwaukee. I couldn't help thinking to myself as I drove towards Milwaukee in a state of shock, how do you look someone in the eyes, and tell them that you will see them soon, knowing that in reality, most likely, it's last time you will ever see them?"

"Wow, it's fortunate that you went to see your dad after dropping your son off at his camp," Pistis said.

"I know. Once again it was because I followed a nudge that Monica and I had better go see him. I just couldn't believe that in only weeks he went from cutting his grass and joking with the waitress over dinner, to lying in the Intensive Care Unit.

We got back home after leaving my dad and started to get Sabrina ready to move into her apartment, which meant she was really moving away from home this time. My world as I knew it was about to radically change. My whole world had revolved around Sabrina, Monica, and Sam. Sabrina and I had done so much together, and now she was moving away for good.

The crazy part was, as I prepared myself to move Sabrina into her new apartment, I had no idea it was about to become one of the worst weeks of my life.

Sabrina was getting ready to move into her new apartment, and my dad lay in a hospital in Indianapolis fighting for his life. Inside I was a total mess.

As I packed up the van with all of Sabrina's things, many different emotions flowed through me. I was angry, sad, and very much confused.

All I knew was that Sabrina needed to be moved into her new apartment in Columbus. And, even though I wasn't ready for Sabrina to leave, the only saving grace was that we were going to stop by and check in on my dad on our way to there.

All week since we got back from the hospital, I longed to be with my dad, and soon we would all be together. I quickly and steadfastly loaded the van with Sabrina's stuff and everything else we needed for the trip. Finally, the moment came; the van was fully loaded.

There was no turning back now. My little girl was about to be on her own. Sure, the last couple of years she was away at school living in the dorms, but she came back on breaks and for the summer. Now, she was moving into an apartment.

Everyone got into the van. I climbed into the driver's seat fighting back tears as it all hit me. My little girl was really moving away this time! I would have given anything to be able to roll the clock back just one more year. Just as I started to pull out of the drive heading towards Indianapolis, my phone rang. Reluctantly, I answered it. As I said hello, Carol said 'Sam your dad just went to be with the Lord.'

'Wait, what? He went where? No, that can't be. We are on our way there now to see you two. No! How? Why? We will there in just a few hours, tell him to wait.'

'Sorry Sam, your dad is gone,' Carol replied.

The van rolled to a stop. I just sat there in shock. No, it couldn't be. He wouldn't leave without saying good-bye, would he? He knew I would be back today. I told him so just last week. So many emotions washed over me. It felt like time quickly flew by. Everyone in the van knew that I was on the phone with Carol.

All eyes were fixed on me as I just leaned over the steering wheel and broke down. 'What just happened?' Jennifer asked. I have never been one to let my emotions get the best of me in front of our kids, so she knew the news I had just heard had to be very bad. I sat there in silence as I tried to regain my composure. Looking up and wiping tears away from my eyes, I said, 'Dad just died.' Silence filled the van.

If we were going to make it around Chicago before rush hour, we needed to quickly get going. So, I put the van in gear, and we started on our journey. I drove as everyone sat there in complete silence. I kept driving as thought after thought rushed through my mind. The remainder of the trip was pretty much quiet except for the occasional story about my dad.

We got to Columbus and moved Sabrina into her new apartment. Later that day, we headed back to Indianapolis. Carol knew that after moving Sabrina into her new apartment, we were headed back to Milwaukee, so she sped things up and arranged my dad's funeral for the next day so we could all be there. My sister was even able to drive down from northern Wisconsin to be there.

We walked into the church and the senior pastor said that my dad was ready to be seen. With an annoyed look on my face, I said, 'Great there is so much I want to ask him.' He looked confused and said, 'I'm sorry, I meant that he is ready, so you can see him.'

'See him; I don't want to SEE him. I want to play cards with him, tell him about Sabrina's new apartment, or discuss why he needs to beat his cancer, so he can come to the twins' high school graduation. If he's not ready to do that, then what is there to see?' I then told him that we didn't want to see him lying in a casket.

We were there to say goodbye, but we wanted to remember him as he was alive. He asked Jennifer and the kids to stay behind and asked me to follow him. As I followed him to the front of the church, I stood there in complete disbelief, as I looked down on my dad laid out there in a casket. I had just said I didn't want to see him this way. Yet there he was. I still can't get the image of him lying there out of my mind. I walked up to what was once my father, picked up his hand, as tears started streaming down my cheeks, and said, 'Dad you have always been my hero,

I grew up feeling like I was alone, Then, over the last few years we really started to connect.

Monica and I had just come to see you and you looked great. Yes, you got sick again and had to go into the hospital for a couple of days. But when we came to see you there, outside of being tired you seemed fine. Over the last week I would wake up wondering where you were. Why would you leave without saying goodbye?' It didn't make any sense.

I knew that God was in control, none-the-less, tears streamed down my face. Why dad? Why God? Why now? Sabrina was starting her third year of college and had just moved into her first apartment. My life as I knew it was about to radically change. I wasn't ready to say goodbye. There was still so much left that I wanted to say. I was so angry. It didn't make any sense. Why did God take my dad at a time when the kids and I truly needed him? Then again … who was I to question God?

Just then it hit me. I had two appointments scheduled for 9:00am and it was now 8:50am; one with Dave and another with Chris I was supposed to be there for those appointments. But by the time I got the phone call it was too late to call them and tell them I wasn't going to be there. I just let my dad's hand fall back to his chest, turned around, left the church, and called them. I told them what happened and that I was sorry that I couldn't be there.

Once again, I was overtaken with emotion. Why now? I had been looking forward to calling my dad and telling him about the two appointments, and how it was the first time I had two recruiting appointments at the same time since I started working for the firm. It was at that point that I realized my first coach, my childhood hero, was gone.

God for whatever reason called him home and he was gone. I walked back into the church, sat down next to my family, and the service began. I was asked to go up and give his eulogy. What could I possibly say in front of all of his friends and family? They needed their own form of closure. I was still so angry at him for once again leaving me at a point when I felt like I needed him most.

I got up, walked up in front of the church, looked out at everyone who was there for him, and knew then that it wasn't about me or how I felt. I was his son. I had to become the strong steward that he tried to raise me to become. This was his moment - his moment to shine. I stood there looking down at him. For whatever reason, the pastor forgot to close the casket. I then spoke out as if I was talking to him. It was as if for one brief moment, my dad and I were the only two people in the room.

'Dad, I'm not sure why you chose this moment to return home, or why God decided to call you home, but you will always be my hero, and a part of you will always be by my side. I will continue to strive to be the steward you raised me to be. I promise I will make you proud. I look forward to the day that we will be together once again. And, I'm sure there will be many new stories to share. Everyone that I am fortunate enough to be able to bless will also be blessed by you. I am a part of you. Your work will be carried through me. I only ask that you continue to watch over me.' Wiping tears away from my eyes, I sat back down next to my family."

"To lose one's father is hard under normal circumstances, but for it to happen the same day your daughter moved away from home makes it doubly hard.

Sam, you have always had such a strong inner guide, and trust in your walk with God. If anything, I would have thought you would be overconfident because you have overcome so much," Pistis said

"The funny thing is every time my business or something in my life reached a certain level of growth it would also hit a glass ceiling. No matter what I would try, I could never break through it. I was stuck!

Over time, I figured out that a big obstacle was a belief I developed as a child that to make a lot of money was bad. Then, coupling that with my poor self-esteem, I was always fighting an uphill battle."

"It's interesting that you have overcome so many obstacles over the years that would stop most people, yet you claim to have poor self-esteem," Pistis said smiling.

"I guess it's because when it comes to overcoming a personal challenge, I fully believe that with Christ behind me and in His timing (the opening of yet another door) all things are possible."

"And how is that different from growing your business? Don't you believe the vision of your dream business, as you put it, came to you from God?" Pistis asked.

"I guess because that involves leading people to join in my vision for the business. That's where the self-confidence comes in. If I'm asking people to pay for the training who already having money challenges, it's like taking candy from a child. I feel like I should first help them, then once they have more money, it would be okay to charge them."

"You see Sam, that's the problem with the word self-esteem or self-confidence. They start with SELF. I suggest you change the word to God esteem or God confidence. You claimed to have poor self-esteem, yet you claimed to fully trust in your walk with God. I would argue that you really have poor God confidence, otherwise you would move forward knowing and believing that God is behind you. Always remember to let go & let God."

"But I would often put it to prayer. I would move forward trying to build the business. My challenge was in asking people for money who clearly were struggling with money."

"Sam, that is a very noble goal or belief if you're already financially independent. But it seems to me that you are still trying to build your own financial foundation."

"I know, that has been a continual challenge. Even though I have been able to help a lot of people over the years, my business keeps falling farther and farther behind. Fortunately, Jennifer's business has been very stable. However, that has put a lot of stress on her," I answered letting out a slight sigh.

"It's great that your heart is so big, but in order for you to grow your business to the degree you want, you are going to need a strong financial foundation. So, it's very important that you watch your time and create systems that can help those who can't afford to pay what you need, without taking up too much of your time.

That is also why it's so important for you to stay focused on the end game and attract people into your business who are able to help you. Right now, in order for you to take your business to the next level, it's going to require the help of many other people. So, for now I would recommend that you look for people who need your help and are able to pay you a fair wage for your help. And at the same time, keep looking for people who can help you grow the business. Does that make sense?"

"Yes, it does."

"In any case, it's time that you learn to harness your God-given gifts and claim the ministry that God has been preparing you for all these years," Pistis said with a large smile.

As the plane touched down in Seattle, the pilot came over the intercom welcoming us into Seattle, thanked us again for choosing to fly with Delta and wished us a safe and wonderful day.

Thanking me for the great conversation, Pistis looked at me with a large smile saying "Remember Sam you are very close to seeing great things happen in your business. Just stay focused and trust that God will continue to lead the way."

"Thanks, Pistis for all your advice and encouragement. I'm so happy that we were able to sit together. One might even say that our sitting together was an answer to prayer."

As we walked up the jet way and into the airport, Pistis turned to the right and as I turned to the left, Pistis looked back and said remember Sam to Let Go and Let God lead the way and He will always be by your side."

"Thanks, Pistis, I will" I replied. As I started to walk towards baggage claim, I turned back once more and Pistis no where to be seen.

Consult not your fears but your hopes and your dreams. Think not about your frustrations, but about your unfulfilled potential. Concern yourself not with what you tried and failed in, but with what is still possible for you to do. Pope John XXIII

Consider it pure joy, my brothers and sisters, whenever you face trials of many kinds, because you know that the testing of your faith produces perseverance. Let perseverance finish its work so that you may be mature and complete, not lacking anything.
- James 1:1-2

CHAPTER 13

Finally Meeting My Silent Mentor

I was sitting on the dock next to a small lake where I was staying, looking out over the water with tears streaming down my cheeks. This was the last day that I would be there. My friends had sold their house. I would be bringing the last of my stuff back to Milwaukee. I kept thinking about how I had worked so hard the last few years yet had nothing to show for it.

Choking back tears, I cried out in a state of total frustration, Are you there, Lord? It is I Lord! Can you hear me? I am here Lord! Are you still with me Lord? I am waiting for your direction! Please grace me with your favor Lord and show me what to do.

"Yes Sam, He is with you." Opening my eyes, I looked up in complete amazement to find Pistis standing there right in front of me. With a caring smile, Pistis looked at me and said, "Sam you did your best given all that has happened to you over the last few years, so stop blaming yourself. Let go of this huge sense of failure you're carrying around and become the person you're meant to be."

"Pistis, how is it that you know these things? And where did you come from?"

"How is it that you do not?"

"Sam remember the story your mom told you about when you were two years old and crawling around under the table near where your mom and sister where watching TV while playing cards. You unplugged the TV from the extension cord and stuck the end that was still connected to the wall into your mouth."

"Yeah I do. But how do you know about that story? I never told you about it," I said with a puzzled look on my face.

"Sam, what happened after you stuck the cord into your mouth?"

"Well according to the story that I was told, my heart stopped, and I laid there on the floor twitching. John ran into the room as my mom and sister started yelling my name. He grabbed me, pounded on my chest and started doing CPR until my heart started beating again. They then rushed me to the hospital."

"Well Sam, that is when you and I first met."

"Wait, what? You were at the hospital?" I blurted out.

Shaking his head and chuckling, Pistis said,

"No Sam, those few moments when your heart stopped, you started to return home. I was sent to interject; it wasn't your time yet. It was at that point that I became your silent mentor I have been with you or behind you ever since."

"The voice I hear behind me at times, my invisible friend, that's you?" I asked starting to tear up.

"Yes Sam, I'm your silent mentor, Pistis said with a large smile.

"No wonder," I said, chuckling.

"No wonder what?"

"Remember when I told you about when I was at the independent school, the school psychologist had me read like twenty different books on psychology. Well, I had this huge fascination with any book I could find at the time that talked about people who had near death experiences."

"That makes sense. It was a hard time in your life, and you were searching for answers. When you came across those books, your subconscious started to make certain connections to the stories you were reading. Part of you still remembered your own near-death experience. That is why you have always had a deep feeling of inner peace, or strong faith as you put it, when it didn't make sense for you to do so," Pistis answered.

"Why are you telling me this now?"

"Sam, it's time for you to evolve into the leader you're designed to be. Yet you're still holding on to certain false and very powerful limiting beliefs that you need to let go of, or they will continue to hold you back. After your children went off to college and you finished the truck driving course, you seemed to be so close to reaching a true state of awareness, yet you were still very disconnected from your God-given purpose.

You have been searching for a spiritual teacher for so long instead of going to the source through prayer. Lately, you have been journaling a lot and you appear to be closest to God when you're flying, so that seemed to be the perfect place to have a personal man to man conversation with you. I sat next to you on the flight from Milwaukee to Minneapolis that day to get a better sense of what your intentions were. But then after listening to you on that flight, I knew you were trying to do what you believed to be the right thing.

I could also tell that you were deeply conflicted from a heart level about which path to take. Should you follow your passion and drive a truck for a while, putting everything else on hold, or should you continue to build your dream business even though it feels like it's been a complete failure? I got the sense that you were at a point where you really needed a friend, someone who would just sit and listen to your story while giving you guiding feedback. I then made a few changes so I could sit next to you again on The Flight to Seattle."

"Wait, you made changes so you could sit next to me on The Flight to Seattle. The flight was full, how did you get the seat right next to me at the last minute?" I asked once again with a puzzled look on my face.

"It helps to have friends in high places," Pistis answered laughing, "Hence my point about what you were calling a coincidence that day on the flight to Seattle.

Anyway, you have come so far on your own. But now it's time for you to take all that you have been taught, all that you have learned, and bring your dream business or community to life. In order to do so, I believe you need to fully understand what your true purpose is. You have reached a point where the only thing standing in your way is your own confidence in your ability to fulfill that dream.

So, Sam, you ask why now? It's simple. I'm telling you this now so you can completely and fully believe that you are not alone. It's important that you continue to build your dream enterprises. I will always be by your side. Through our different discussions, you have asked some really good questions, and you have many stories that demonstrate the true power of staying true to one's faith, even when all things seemed impossible. It's time for you to share those stories with others so they too can find their own faith and stay true to their own calling. It's for that reason I came to you today."

"Pistis, the one thing I still don't understand, is all the signs pointed to my being drawn back to Seattle so I could help Robert and Ron build an office in Seattle. Even though I came here every other week for the past three years, I feel like it's been a complete waste of time and money. Not to mention all the time I spent away from Jennifer and the kids," I said with a long sigh, fighting back tears.

"Sam, remember on the plane to Seattle when you shared with me that you believed God brought Sabrina into Robert's life through Toastmasters as an anchor to bring him into the financial business, then ten years later brought you and Robert together again so you two could open an office together? You said you were getting flak from other people because you weren't getting results in Seattle, so you should stop going there. Yet, you believed that it was God's will for you to stay in Seattle and continue to help Robert until the office became a success. And, many times you cried out in prayer wondering if that was truly God's purpose, why then were you having so many difficulties?"

"Yes," I responded.

"Sam, remember the parable of 'Law of the Talents'. I shared how the parable talked about people's God-given talents. Now I'm going to refer to a talent as a unit of value. If I give you one talent, according to the parable, what should you do with that talent?"

"I should invest that talent so that it will grow in value," I answered.

"Correct. Now let's go three years back when you were invited to attend the Peak Experience retreat. Let's assume that the invitation was God giving you a talent or unit of value."

"But the invitation didn't have value attached to it. In fact, I had to pay in-order to go," I blurted out.

"The invitation didn't have any value attached to it?" Pistis said with an annoyed tone. Sam, isn't it true that you had secretly wanted to attend the retreat ever since you picked your client up from the airport many years back, who had just attended the Peak Experience retreat, and she told you how awesome it was?"

"Yeah, I guess."

"Can *anyone* attend the event?"

"No, it's by invitation only," I answered.

"So, the invitation does carry with it an intangible value. Even if you had lots of money, without the invitation you still wouldn't be able to attend the event, right Sam?"

"Yeah, that's true; a person still has to be invited. I did wish I could go for a few years before I was invited, and I was really happy when I got the invitation. But still, at the time it took a huge leap of faith to go," I said.

"True Sam, you knew you couldn't afford it, yet you went anyway out of faith. So, God gave you the talent, the invitation, and you had to make a choice. Take the invitation and make the investment to go, or you could have turned down the invitation out of fear and buried the talent in the ground. Because you went, you met Ron who then introduced you to Sarah, and together you were able to open the office in Tacoma. Plus, haven't you and Ron and Sarah also become friends? One might say that was a pretty good return on your money," Pistis said chuckling.

"Very true, but I still can't help feeling like these past few years have been a galactic failure."

"Why do you say that?"

"I guess because if it's true that God brought me into Robert's life to help him build a branch office, then I have greatly failed him."

"Really Sam? You failed who, Robert or God? Pistis asked.

"I guess both."

"Ok, let's first examine disappointing God.

If you had to pick one, what would you say is your greatest fear?"

"Oh, that's easy. Flying!"

"Flying?!" Pistis asked in disbelief.

"Yep, flying. When I was really young, we took my mom to the airport for a trip, and she had a panic attack because of her own fear of flying and almost didn't get on the plane. I guess that had a lingering effect on me. Plus, I don't like being off the ground. That is why I like to sit in the window seat.

If I can at least see the ground it helps with the fear. Plus, when I look out over the horizon, it almost feels like I'm sitting in God's front yard. As I look out across the wide-open sky, it almost feels like I'm sitting there in the palm of God's hand," I said.

"Yet Sam, wouldn't you say you fly pretty often?"

"Yeah, I fly back and forth between Milwaukee and Seattle every two weeks at a minimum and have done so over the past two-and-a-half years. I probably logged a quarter of million miles in the air."

"Yet Sam, you say your greatest fear is flying?"

"Yep, that would be correct."

"But why do you do it? Most people try to avoid their fears."

"Like I told you on the plane; at first, I started going to Seattle because I thought the kids wanted to go to school there, and because I really liked being in Seattle. Every time I put it to prayer, God opened another door making it easier for me.

But really the day when Robert and I were talking, and he told me about how Sabrina had impacted him, I truly believed that my going to Seattle and helping Robert and Ron build a footprint there was somehow Gods providence. If that's the case, who am I to let my fear of flying get in the way?"

"What a great example of staying true to your faith." Pistis said, laughing.

"Yeah, I guess so," I replied with a slight sigh.

"What Sam? You don't sound so sure."

"I guess Pistis, I just wish I had more results to show is all."

"Sam, what would you say is your next greatest fear?"

"I guess not being around for the kids. I have always been there for them. I always made sure that I didn't let the business get in the way of Jennifer or me spending quality time with them," I answered.

"Ok, so it seems to me, Sam, that being in Seattle so much the last few years would have in a way made that difficult."

"Yeah, there were many days that I really missed them and wished I was with them."

"Were they then left alone?"

"No, Jennifer ran her business from home, so she was there with them. Plus, they were really busy with high school."

"Yeah Sam but wasn't Jennifer always there?"

"No, I guess that was one good thing about my being in Seattle so much over the last couple of years. Because I planned my business around their school activities, I was always there when they needed me. So, Jennifer was able to focus on building her business and didn't spend as much time with them."

"How did that work out for everyone?"

"In many ways I could feel a distance between Jennifer and the kids as they got older, but because I was in Seattle so much, it forced them to reconnect and have a deeper relationship now," I said.

"So even though you feared not being there, you went anyway because you believed it was God's calling for you. At the end of the day, not being around as much turned out to be a good thing now that you look back on it."

"Yeah, I guess you're right."

"Still, Sam at the time you didn't know that, yet you still choose to go to Seattle every other week even though it was tearing you up inside. Why?" Pistis asked.

"Simple, because I truly believed that it was God's calling for me, and if I stayed faithful to his calling, he would help with what I was trying to build."

"And did He?"

"I don't know. My business hasn't really grown, and I don't really feel like I have been able to help Robert grow the office. That's why I feel like I let him down," I answered.

"OK Sam, how about your living arrangements while you were in Seattle? How did that work out?"

"Well, at first I stayed in different hotels. Then, some good friends and real estate clients of mine wanted to sell their house. The real estate market had fallen, so they weren't able to get what they needed if they sold it. I suggested that they rent the house out, and I could stay in a room above a two-car detached garage to keep an eye on things when I was in Seattle. They could take some time off and spend a year in their RV in the southwest while they waited for the real estate market to rebound," I answered.

"That sounds like it was pretty good advice, and it was probably better than staying in different hotels. So, how did it work out?"

"Overall it wasn't bad. The room was 20 feet by 30 feet, had a small heater, a small refrigerator, and TV in it. The only thing it was lacking was a bathroom. Monica often referred to the room as the hut. I used the bathroom at a grocery store that was about a mile away. Plus, there was a park at the end of the road that had a bathroom I could use if need be.

I then took showers at a nearby health club. So, all in all it wasn't bad. In fact, the strange thing is that even though I often complained about staying there because it could be very lonely; now that they sold the property, I'm going to miss the hut. In fact, I often dreamed about buying it even though I knew it wasn't very practical."

"So, did your friends end up finally being able to sell the house?"

"Yep, and because they waited to sell their house, they were able to get $200,000 more for it than if they had sold it two years prior. The funny thing is the amount they got for the property ended up being what they needed to really retire and do the things that they wanted to do."

"So, staying in the hut, as you call it, gave you a place to call home when you were in Seattle and helped them not have to sell the property at a much lower price."

"Yep, that's correct."

"Who helped them sell the house?"

"Ron did."

"Did he charge them the full commission?"

"Nope. Because of our relationship, Ron only charged fifty percent of what he would have normally charged, which helped them get the amount they really needed."

"So, because you were in Seattle, you were able to help Ron and his business, and you were able to really help your friends. As it is written in James 2:14-17, 'What good is it my brothers and sisters if someone claims to have faith, but has no deeds? Can such faith save them? Suppose a brother or a sister is without clothes and daily food. If one of you says to them, 'Go in peace, keep warm and well fed' but does nothing about their physical needs, what good is it? In the same way, faith by itself, if it is not accompanied by action, is dead.' Or another of my favorites, John 15:13, 'Greater love has no more than this: to lay one's life for one's friends.' If you hadn't suggested that they rent out the main house and you would stay in the garage and keep an eye on things, would they have been able to travel and wait another two years before selling the house?"

"I don't know, probably not."

"It seems to me that you were trying to help your friends realize as much as they could for their house. Plus, didn't you give them money for staying in the hut and didn't ask for any money when it came time to sell the house?" Pistis asked with a large smile.

"Yeah, but for me it was never about making money. I just wanted to help my friends realize as much as they could for selling their house."

"Sam, I can't think of a better way for you to honor God's will than that."

"Pistis, if that's the case, then why didn't God help me with growing the Bellevue office? If I was there to help Robert, why didn't God show favor towards us? I hate flying, yet I flew to Seattle every two weeks for almost three years. I hated being away from Jennifer and the kids, yet I still went. Don't even get me started with the hut! Why do I have to look Jennifer, the kids, and my co-workers in the eyes, knowing that I have no production to show for all my efforts?" I snapped back, with tears starting to run down my cheeks.

"Sam, what is it that you're basing your level of production on? Your so-called production may have been way off, however you remained a faithful steward to what you believed God's mission was for you.

What is considered a failure to one person often isn't failure to someone else. One might argue that true failure is to become very good at doing the wrong thing. Focusing only on activities that are not part of one's personal mission. The activities of the heart may not seem like society's definition of success, but that's okay. The greater question is what's in your heart truly God's will for you? If so, then success will come in God's time. That may be different than what you may want or expect. In the end, if you follow your heart, God will guide you to ultimate success. It is at that point that you will truly become His disciple; not on your grounds, rather on His.

"You know that has always been my desire, Pistis, yet I still feel like I failed all who have put their trust in me."

If honoring God is truly your wish, then you're on the right path. That's why it's so important to find solitude, time to relax, and listen to the calls of the heart. God is always guiding people, but because they aren't paying attention, they will often not notice it, or assume it's something else.

People often have a false sense of pride from accomplishing certain things. However, if for some reason they aren't able to reach their expected level of success, they will look for an excuse as to why they weren't able to accomplish it and will feel like a failure.

There is a very fine line between pride and self-pity. The underlying difference is that pride has the ability to empower you to move past powerful challenges, whereas self-pity will enable you to stay stuck, excuse away the need for dealing with the challenge, and justify your actions in the name of pride.

Similar to that of complaining, people often complain about a problem because they recognize the issue and know that something needs to be done to ratify the problem. But it's not bad enough that they are willing to face the challenge head-on and resolve the issue. Instead, they complain about it. By complaining, they feel like they are addressing the issue without making things too uncomfortable.

So, Sam, if God is the true source of your light, wouldn't it only make sense that He would continue to shine a bright light for you to follow? And, if the light of God illuminates the way, what is there to fear? This is where fear stops, and faith takes over. The problem is that most people are not willing to trust Him completely.

Think back to the days of Adam and Eve. It was God's will for us to live in paradise. True, the snake came along and messed things up, but wouldn't it be fair to say that God still wants us to live in Paradise? It's people that keep messing things up. Sam, you have an amazing sense of inner strength and courage. However, you still need to work on following your heart. That's where you will find God's guidance."

"Yeah, but I still feel like I let Robert down!" I said with a long sigh.

"Sam let's go back roughly three years ago, right before you started going to Seattle on a more frequent basis. Do you remember Jennifer getting mad and saying that maybe you two should get a divorce? That she wanted to go back to Taiwan? That no one cared if she was there anyways? Or the afternoon when Jennifer called Sabrina at school, crying, and said she wanted to leave and go back to Taiwan, that she felt tired and invisible?

"Yes, I was listening on the other line, even though she didn't know I was on the line," I answered, once again puzzled that Pistis knew this.

"How did you feel, when you heard her say that?"

"I don't know? Hurt that she felt that way, and in some ways like a failure as a husband. A husband is supposed to make his wife feel stable, happy, comfortable, and loved. She felt none of that at the time. I thought I was working hard to build a good life for Jennifer and the kids. I knew Jennifer's job was really important to her, so I thought if I built my business while taking care of the kids, it would be the perfect situation. I was in shock at how Jennifer could be telling Sabrina those things. Sabrina didn't need to hear about it. I was confused. Why would she think the kids or I didn't need her around?

I may have been the main parent figure at the time, but our kids needed their mother around.

I knew no matter what, getting divorced wasn't the answer. I remember thinking that maybe if I moved out and got an apartment that might help. But that seemed like a large step towards getting a divorce. Our kids' friends, neighbors, the world would all be on notice that we were having marriage problems. Plus, it was very important to me that we kept the family unit together. I just fell into a state of depression. My world was unraveling right there in front of me. And, I once again didn't understand why God was doing this to me when I was trying to do what I believed to be the right thing.

My business was in limbo. I clearly needed to find a different market to work in. I felt like a fish out of water in Milwaukee. I kept thinking, 'If only I had stayed in Seattle'. Sabrina was off at college. The twins were busy in high school and would soon go off to college themselves. Jennifer didn't seem to want me around. I had just found out that my dad had pancreatic cancer and had only about six months to live. Then there was Robert out in Seattle who seemed to need my help there.

I remember once again finding myself on my knees asking God for guidance and feeling this incredible sense of direction come over me. If I spent part of the time in Seattle, I could help Robert grow the office there. It would give Jennifer and me the space that she seemed to need, and I would be back in a market that I understood. I still had a lot of friends and clients in Seattle who could help me grow the business. So, I booked a flight to Seattle and a week later I was there," I explained.

"Then what happened Sam?"

"Well, I still had doubts about whether or not I was doing the right thing. However, things seemed to be falling into place. Then, as I was sharing with you on the flight, when Robert told me the story about Sabrina and Toastmasters, I knew that I truly was doing God's will."

"Sam, once you started going to Seattle on a frequent basis, did you and Jennifer begin to get along better?"

"Yeah Pistis, surprisingly that was the last time she talked about leaving and we didn't argue as much when I was back in Milwaukee."

"I know that you said you often felt lonely and homesick when you were staying in the hut, but wouldn't it be fair to say, that being alone so much forced you to reconnect with your inner self?"

"Yeah, I guess you have a point. Before I started going to Seattle so much, my life was totally wrapped around the kids. In many ways over the years, I had lost my own identity. Yet, being in Seattle allowed me to find myself again."

"And, wouldn't it be fair to say that being in Seattle so much the last couple of years may very well have saved your marriage?" Pistis asked.

"Yeah it may have; it certainly didn't hurt it. It has been a crazy couple of years though. Between my dad dying on the same day that I moved Sabrina into her first apartment, and knowing that Jennifer and I were going to soon become empty nesters; in a way, I really needed the time by myself to work through everything. I was a total mess for a while. I tried to keep a brave exterior, like everything was still ok. But there were many days that I felt like crawling into a hole and dying."

"Wow! That sounds like a lot for anyone to handle and would likely slow most people down. So, Sam, to recap; your being in Seattle allowed you to help your friends with their house which will allow them to have a much better retirement, most likely saved your marriage, forced Jennifer and the kids to reconnect so now they have a much better relationship, and probably kept Jennifer from moving back to Taiwan, or in with her sister and leaving everyone. Oh, and you helped bring Ron and Sarah into Global View Capital Advisors, which in time will allow them to help many people reach financial independence. Plus, it seems to me that your being in Seattle the last couple of years helped you grow into the leader you need to be in order to really bring your dream business into reality. Does that sound like a fair assessment?"

"Yeah, I guess I never really looked at it like that. I have been so focused on trying to help Roger develop the Seattle base.

"Sam would you agree that Robert is a true servant or shepherd for God?"

"Yes, he is one of the godliest people I know."

That's why I thought it was so amazing that through Sabrina, God brought Robert and me together, which again is why I feel so bad for not being able to do a better job at helping him," I said.

"Sam, you just said that over the last couple of years, your oldest daughter left home and went away to college, you lost your father to cancer, your marriage was falling apart, the twins were becoming more distant with Jennifer, even to the degree that she was thinking that no one would care if she left, and that there were many days when you felt like crawling into a hole and dying. Yet because you have been going to Seattle so much, you were able to work through all of that, and in fact, now things have turned out pretty good? It seems to me that you have things backwards."

"Backwards! What do you mean?"

"Sam you feel bad, because you haven't been able to help Roger as much, so you let both God and Robert down. Isn't that was you said earlier?"

"Yeah, I guess so."

"Well Sam, as I said, maybe you have it backwards; that in fact, God used Sabrina to plant an anchor that would later bring Robert into your life at a time when you needed a friend, a business partner, a spiritual mentor, and a reason to spend so much time in Seattle. You see, without Robert coming into your life, all the things we just talked about still would have happened, except the outcome may have been a lot worse.

Most likely your marriage would have fallen apart, and Jennifer and the kids would have become even more distant. They may have even blamed you for letting it all fall apart and stopped talking to you as well. Jennifer most likely would have moved back to Taiwan or in with her sister, leaving everyone. You very likely would have slipped into a serious state of depression.

Chances are your friends wouldn't have realized as much for their house when they sold it, which would have kept them from being able to have as comfortable a retirement. Oh, and you wouldn't have met Ron and brought him and Sarah into Global View Capital Advisors. I don't know how things would have turned out Sam, but I am willing to bet that things would be a lot different, and probably not for the better. You can't always understand why, or when, God does what He does. That is why it's so important to stay true to your faith. If you continue to listen for His guidance, He will always show you the way at the right time.

The one thing I do know, Sam, is the reason that I'm here in front of you now is because it's time for you to rise up and become the leader, teacher, and shepherd that God has designed you to be. The next couple of years are going to bring some significant changes, and the need for your vision or dream business is necessary now more than ever. So, grab a hold of your destiny, and create the ultimate business community." Pistis then turned and walked up the path, disappearing into the trees.

Watching Pistis disappear into the trees, I sat there in complete silence as I digested everything he had just told me. I couldn't help thinking to myself that if the last 14 years truly were laid out by God's design, then all the different things I had done over the last fourteen years should fit together like a puzzle. I then picked up my pen and note pad and mapped out the last fourteen years, since the final part of my vision was revealed to me on my 40th birthday.

Writing out the last fourteen years was like watching my life unravel right there in front of my eyes. On one hand, it all made perfect sense. I knew exactly what I needed to do, yet on the other hand, I still felt so lost. <u>Check out the epilogue to see how it all fits together.</u>

As I started to regain my composure, I said goodbye to the lake, goodbye to the house, stood up, and walked over to where my suitcase sat. Putting it in the car, I wiped tears away and turned as I said goodbye to the hut. Getting into my car, I headed up the street, bringing that chapter of my life to an end. As I reached the top of Snoqualmie Pass, I smiled knowing I was just 1,900 miles away from the start of another adventure.

Epilogue

As I sit here, I'm thinking about the conversation between Sam and Pistis that morning down by the dock and the magnitude of the mission now in front of me. On one hand, I can't help but feel a great sense of excitement. On the other hand, I am in many ways terrified. I know what I need to do. The parts I'm still not sure about continue to become revealed to me. As I continue to grow into the leader that God has designed me to be, it's becoming more and more apparent that the other leaders and people needed to bring my vision to the next level and beyond are coming into my life each and every day.

I'm currently sitting here 23 stories above the very lobby where I made the decision as a twelve-year-old to devote my life to becoming an entrepreneur and going to work on my vision, which has been a life-long journey since. Looking down at the building and its lobby, I can't help asking myself was it just the law of attraction, or God's design for me to end up owning a condo kitty-corner from that building's lobby? I write this 41 years after the morning I made that commitment to God to somehow, some way design an entrepreneurial movement that seemed so needed even back then.

When I find myself second-guessing my vision or asking, 'who am to build such an enterprise?', the words of Eleanor Roosevelt come to mind. 'He who loses money loses much, He who loses a friend loses much more, He who loses faith loses all.'

Throughout this book, I have shared many of the stories and lessons that led up to this point, and how at times when things seemed way out of my reach, God opened a much-needed door and the solution would appear. I shared how through faith, determination, and hard work; we can climb the highest mountains. 'By the Grace of God go I.'

Sitting here looking out the window, I still can't help asking myself, "How much of this vision is my own passion to go out and make a positive difference in the world, and how much is really outside of my range of possibility, and truly God-driven guidance?"

Here is the map that I wrote down in my notebook on the dock the last day I was at the hut. This is what it looked like:

- October 2004: I had a vision of the final series of puzzle pieces needed to design a powerful movement for bringing financial management and succession planning solutions to the small business owner, average investor, children, and beyond.

- March 2005: I received a strong God-given nudge to sell our house and business, then move back to Milwaukee. Jennifer gave me a 30-day window to pull it all together or she wasn't going. I told her that 30 days was too short, and she told me that if it was truly God's divine intervention, then He would make it happen. After putting it to prayer and asking for God's help, he delivered all the pieces needed to make it happen, and we received a full-price offer on our house by the 29th day.

- May 2005: my daughter Sabrina gave a presentation at Toastmasters talking about the importance of teaching financial management to children. That was the last Toastmasters meeting we went to in Seattle.

- The summer of 2005 to 2007: Sabrina and I wrote our first book which became the beginning of the Centsible Solutions series.

- The end of 2007: I found myself on my knees one night crying out to God and asking for guidance. I prayed that if I was really supposed to build out my vision, for Him to open the door needed for that to happen.

- The next morning: Chris decided at the last minute to go a Toastmasters meeting even though he was really busy at the office and wasn't going to go. I was supposed to give a speech that day on goal setting but got a strong nudge to change my speech one minute before I was supposed to give it to "The Importance of Financial Planning," and just got up and spoke from my heart. Chris was so moved by the speech that he invited me to an open house at his office that night and introduced me to Dave and Dona. The next day I joined their firm.

- August 2010: I attended a large real estate convention and listened to the president of CRS talk about the importance of building a community within the real estate industry. The next day I woke up with a vision of creating real estate and financial teams, or hubs, around the country and how that would play into my dream of an entrepreneurship movement.
- The end of 2010: I was at another crossroads. I believed whole-heartedly that Dave and Dona were the mentors I needed to bring my vision to life, yet I couldn't see how it could possibly happen given the current firm we were at. I once again found myself calling out to God for guidance.
- The next day: Dave and Dona called a special meeting and shared their frustrations with us. They said they were going in a different direction. They invited anyone who shared the same mission to follow them. For me, it was an answer to prayer. The next several months were a very trying time for them, yet they stayed true to their vision and never gave up. For that I will be forever grateful.
- October 2011: on my birthday, exactly seven years to the day, Dave and Dona announced that GVCA was free and ready to quickly grow.
- 2013: Robert called Dave and asked to join GVCA.
- 2013: I returned from Vancouver, BC, and Seattle, and told Dave that I had a strong nudge to build an office in Seattle that could also one day serve Canada. He then told me about Robert and that he would be at our annual event.
- One month later: As I pulled up to the event, I prayed that if Robert was the one who could help with Seattle that we would have time to talk at the event. I entered the event which had roughly 120 people there. I looked all over but wasn't able to find Robert, so I found an empty chair and sat down. A few minutes later, after calling his wife and asking her to pray that he would meet someone at the event who could help him open an office in Seattle. Robert entered the room, walked over to where he had previously laid down his binder, sat down next to me, and said, "Hi I'm Robert I'm from Seattle." God works in funny ways!

- Six months later: Robert and I were talking at our office in Seattle. I asked him why he left Boeing and entered the financial industry. He went on to explain that in 2005 he was working as an engineer for Boeing. He was invited to go to a Toastmasters meeting by a friend from church. He heard this ten-year-old girl give a speech on why it was so important for parents to teach their children money management skills. He was so impacted by her speech that he retired from Boeing and went into the financial industry full-time so that he could help with her cause. We then discovered that girl was in fact my daughter, and through Sabrina, God had planted the seed for us to meet eight years prior to our eventual meeting.
- 2014: I was invited to attend the Peak Producers event in San Diego, California which was by invitation only and cost 5,000 dollars to attend. I didn't have 5,000 dollars at the time. It was for real estate leaders who had great businesses, and mine was struggling at best. I had every reason for why I shouldn't be there, yet I was invited. Someone clearly believed that I belonged there.
- After praying for guidance on what I should do, I had this ever-growing sense that I needed to be there. I was able to pull together the 5,000 dollars, but if I went, I wouldn't have enough to make our mortgage payment. On one hand, my going felt so right, yet didn't make any sense. I remember asking God, "Please God if this is truly your will, then just introduce one person to me who can help take my vision to the next level."
- The next morning: I got up, left the house, and flew to San Diego. Arriving at the event, I walked into a conference room with 200 people in it and sat down at a table. We were divided up into groups for the remainder of the event. I sat down next to Ron. Six months later he became part of GVCA.
- 2015: I shared with Ron how part of my vision was to create real estate and financial teams within the coaching community we were part of, and within the real estate industry as a whole. That way, we could help people both

in growing their businesses, real estate, and financial needs. I then planted the seed for building multiple hubs across the US and Canada.

- 2016: I published my second book helping to grow my community.
- 2016: I met with Jim, the CRS past president, who gave the speech I attended at the CRS dinner back in 2010 at a conference. After our meeting, I told him about how his presentation really impressed me and gave him a copy of my book.
- 2017: I got invited to enter a speaking contest by someone who had read my second book. The contest consisted of 20 people who would give a five-minute speech judged by 10 judges. The night before the contest, I woke up in the middle of the night channeling what was to become the winning speech. Two weeks later I was invited to become part of a book collaboration project and became a #1 best-selling author. I am now receiving speaking and writing opportunities on a continual basis.
- January 2018: Ron and two of his teammates spent two days in Milwaukee meeting with Chris, Dave, and Dona discussing how to create real estate and financial teams across the US and Canada.
- March 2018: I once again had coffee with Jim the past CRS president, and his partner. After spending three hours sharing with them about my book, what I was doing at GVCA, and what they were doing with a new real estate company they had just became part of, Jim and his partner became part of GVCA and want to work together to create real estate and financial teams across the US and Canada.
- October 2018: Once again, seven years from the day when Dave and Dona officially announced the birth of GVCA, we were all sitting together listening to Dave and Dona share their vision and reminding us of the incredible road ahead. Except this time, we were sitting at large hotel conference room with a much larger group of advisors from all over the country and Canada. And this time, I was sitting at a table with every one of the key players I just

shared with you who were needed to finally launch my vision.

I can't help but find myself amazed, as today is once again my birthday, bringing the past seven years since GVCA was born to an end. Over the past few weeks I have found myself frequently praying for direction on the path God has put in front of me.

As the timeline shows, I needed to show up and do my part. However, it was God's divine guidance that brought it all together.

Why is this important? Simple. There is a huge need for what we are building. We can help people who are young, nearing retirement, building a small or large business, or are anywhere in-between, live the lives they deserve and live their lives on purpose. I'm a firm believer of the phrase, 'By ourselves we can do great things, yet together we can climb the highest mountains.' I invite you the reader to join us, and together let's design a world that shines with greatness.

As I go back through all these points of interjection, there is one thing that has become extremely clear. Granted, over the years I have become pretty good at attracting things into my life. But Sabrina made an impact on Robert that prepared him to be at a place for us to reconnect eight years later at a time when I greatly needed his presence in my life. I got a nudge to move back to Milwaukee at a time that didn't make any sense because the limousine business was finally doing great.

I was then introduced to Dave and Dona by Chris, who then designed Global View Capital Advisors at a time when people really needed its solutions. I then entered an event and sat next to Ron at a time when he was most receptive to our mission. These stories show the true power of God's continued guidance in our lives if we only let Him. I can't plan for what I can't see or couldn't possibly know.

Over the last two weeks, many of the remaining doors of the past have been closed, clearing the path for what the future has yet to bring. With my birthday drawing to an end, and rolling over into the first day of the next seven year season, I can't help but smile as I sit here in Peterbuilt of Waukesha's parking lot, having just dropped off a truck that not so long ago, I could have only dreamed of driving. Now I know it's the reward for having been a faithful servant trying to follow my God-given purpose.

As I looked at the clock on my dashboard, it changed to 12:01am. I closed my eyes and thanked God for a great birthday. I asked for guidance as I move into the next seven-year journey.

I then picked up my phone and pulled up the website for the program a great friend and coach was telling me about just the day before. Filling out the application, I closed my eyes and prayed for Gods favor. I pushed submit, and I smiled as the welcome massage popped up, knowing that I now held the tool in my hand to launch my vision. I put the car in drive and started to pull forward as the number 100,000,000 jumped out at me. For the first time since I had the vision as a twelve-year-old, I had an actual number for the amount of people my vision should strive to reach. I sat there in complete amazement as I prayed that if it was truly His will, then over the next seven years, we will positively change and improve the lives of one hundred million people allowing us to collectively raise the level of vibration or energy from which those we are blessed to serve resonate from. Through the creation of this entrepreneurial movement, we will be able to truly serve God at a world changing level.

I prayed that with what we are already doing and God's favor behind us, we would be able to help those we are blessed to reach find their own true paths or purpose. As we continue to attract and design the key solutions needed, we will be able to help those we are blessed to work with plan for retirement, build a small business, take an existing business to the next level, and design a solid financial foundation, empowering them to live the lives they deserve.

There is one thing for certain; by staying true to our God-given purposes and continually seeking His guidance, we can achieve great things. Throughout this book, I have shared many stories and examples, and there are many more examples I haven't shared about how God's divine guidance has gone to work in my life, as I'm sure He has in yours as well. It's just whether or not we pay attention to the signs when they present themselves.

I invite you to link arms with us and become a member of our ever-growing community. Together we will make great positive impacts in the lives of those close to us, in our communities, and the world over-all.

I pray that after all these stories, you too can see how God is at work in your life and how He is able to work through you if you will only faithfully watch for His signs and let Him in. Let go, let God, and you too will see his amazing power.

I invite you the reader to pay it forward by thinking about one or two things you learned from the stories I have shared, write down what you learned, and what you can do to improve your own life or the life of someone near you. Next, think of someone who would benefit from this book and please give, loan, or share this book with them.

I invite you to check out our workbook and bible study notes and pray that it may serve as a bible study resource for you and your church. I have also created a series training programs and a key note presentation on discovering the power of Gods grace through staying faithful in His walk.

A song of hope

Here I am Lord
A beautiful song by Donald L Schutte

I the Lord of sea and sky, I have heard my people cry.
I who made the stars of night, I will make their darkness bright.
I the Lord of snow and rain, I have borne my people's pain.
I will break their hearts of stone, Give them hearts for love a lone.
I the Lord of wind and flame, I will tend the poor and lame.
Finest Bread I will provide before their hearts be satisfied.
All who dwell in dark and sin my hand will save.
Who will bear my light in them? I have wept for love of them.
They turn a way. I will speak my word to them.
I will set a feast for them. My hand will save.
I will give my life to them. Whom shall I send?
Whom shall I send? Here I am Lord
Whom shall I send? Is it I Lord? I have heard it calling in the night.
I will go Lord, if you lead me. I will hold your people in my heart.
- Dan Schutte 1981, Donald L Schutte and NALK

Meet the Author

Mike Raber is a # 1 Amazon Bestselling Business Author, Speaker and Coach. Mike's skills and capabilities of leadership, building relationships, growing different businesses and writing a book with his young daughter on the secret to raising financial savvy kids has helped to make him the father and wealth coach that he is today. He offers a bonus of having a real estate, business, insurance and financial planning background.

From years of working and training the youth with his daughter, and working with many different business owners, he has found a great need for programs covering financial management, leadership and business development designed for the many challenges our youth and woman in business face on a daily basis.

In every sense, Mike Raber is a true gentleman. Mike's skills and capabilities of leadership, building relationships, and action may be overlooked by those who don't know him well. Don't be fooled by his subtle approach of care and concern when you engage with this master, for he has it all under control.

Mike has lived boldly in some extreme situations, which has assisted him in refining his approach to people and success. Some of Mike's experiences are filled with shocking and learning moments. He's all too happy to share snippets of his personal and professional journeys – especially learning to optimize Eastern and Western philosophies and practices for better living.

172

You can learn more about Mike, one of our training programs
or Samuel Pistis Ministries at www.thesilentmentor.com

$19.95

ISBN 978-1-7334410-0-1

51995>

9 781733 441001

Made in the USA
Lexington, KY
13 November 2019